AN OUTLINE OF VEDIC LITERATURE

THE AMERICAN ACADEMY OF RELIGION
AIDS TO THE STUDY OF RELIGION SERIES

edited by
M. Gerald Bradford

Number 5

# AN OUTLINE OF VEDIC LITERATURE

by
James A. Santucci

SCHOLARS PRESS
Missoula, Montana

# AN OUTLINE OF VEDIC LITERATURE

by
James A. Santucci

Published by
SCHOLARS PRESS
for

THE AMERICAN ACADEMY OF RELIGION

Distributed by

SCHOLARS PRESS
University of Montana
Missoula, Montana 59801

# AN OUTLINE OF VEDIC LITERATURE

by

James A. Santucci



Library of Congress Cataloging in Publication Data

Santucci, James A
An outline of Vedic literature.

(Aids for the study of religion series; no. 5)
Bibliography: p.
1. Vedic literature—History and criticism. 2. Vedic literature—Bibliography. I. Title. II. Series.
BL1110.S35 294'.1 76-27859
ISBN 0-89130-085-6

Printed in the United States of America

Printing Department
University of Montana
Missoula, Montana 59801

# TABLE OF CONTENTS

FOR WINIFRED

## INTRODUCTION

The term 'Veda' means, in the most general sense, 'knowledge,' that is, the sum of knowledge by which one must understand all the 'arts' and 'sciences' required by the religious life. It is, to be more specific, 'sacred knowledge' or the knowledge of superhuman or godlike powers together with the methods required to influence them. This knowledge grew out of the inspired 'visions' of seers (*ṛ́ṣi*'s) in the remote past--the beginnings of such inspirations perhaps going as far back as 2000 B.C. They belonged in great part to priestly families, who, being the bearers of sacerdotal and esoteric knowledge, transmitted this knowledge within their own circle or 'school': at first orally, and later with the aid of the printed word.

What is now called Vedic literature, however, consists essentially of four classes of composition: *Saṃhitā's*, *Brāhmaṇa's*, *Āraṇyaka's*, and *Upaniṣad's*. These texts have been subjected to intense investigation for well over one-hundred years by hundreds of scholars. Fortunately, a fairly complete bibliography of these works has been compiled by two outstanding Vedic scholars: Louis Renou and R.N. Dandekar. Professor Renou has collected a relatively complete list of those works published up to 1930 and Professor Dandekar has since published three volumes containing a comprehensive list of those writings spanning the years 1930 to 1972 which have the Veda and allied topics as their subject. Bibliographical information concerning these volumes are listed as follows:

Renou, Louis. *Bibliographie Védique*. Paris: Adrien-Maisonneuve, 1931.

Dandekar, R.N. *Vedic Bibliography*. Three Volumes. Volume I [Bombay: Karnatak Publishing House, 1946]; Volume II [Poona: University of Poona, 1961]; Volume III [Poona: Bhandarkar Oriental Research Institute, 1973].

Turning now to the present work at hand, the genesis of the project arose out of a requisite need that developed in a class on Vedic religion taught by me a few years ago. It is designed to answer for the most part basic questions referring to the place, importance, subject matter, together with useful editions, translations, and related works of interest, of each Vedic work. Any errors with regard to the contents, of course, are strictly my own responsibility. Certain omissions with regard to bibliographical information were, unfortunately, unavoidable.

# CHAPTER ONE

## SAṂHITĀ'S (COLLECTIONS)

A. Ṛgveda-Saṃhitā 'The Collection of the Ṛgveda, i.e., the Veda or knowledge of verses, stanzas, or strophes (ṛ́c-).'

The Ṛgveda is the oldest and most important work of Vedic literature. The collection is divided into ten books (Máṇḍala-'circle') consisting of 1,028 hymns (sūktá-), eleven of which were subsequently introduced, called Vālakhilya's (contained in Maṇḍala 8, hymns 49-59). Another arrangement divides the Ṛgveda into eight áṣṭaka's ('eighths'), each of which is subdivided into eight adhyāya's ('chapters' or 'lessons') while each of the latter consists of várga's ('groups') of five or six stanzas. There are 432,000 syllables, 153,826 words, and about 10,000 lines of verse in the text, equivalent in size to the poems of Homer.

The hymns of the Ṛgveda were composed and handed down orally in different families during a period dating from around 1800 B.C. They were gradually brought together over the course of perhaps several hundred years till they assumed the semblance of a collection. Then followed the formation of the Saṃhitā text which occurred around 600 B.C., or approximately at the end of the Brāhmaṇa period. Maṇḍalas two to seven constitute the Family Books, that is, the hymns contained in each of these books constitute compositions of various members of the same family. Thus the second Maṇḍala is devoted to the compositions of the Gṛtsamada family, the third Maṇḍala to the Viśvāmitra family, the fourth Maṇḍala to the Vāmadeva family, the fifth Maṇḍala to the Atri family, the sixth Maṇḍala to the Bharadvāja family, and the seventh Maṇḍala to the Vasiṣṭha family. These Maṇḍalas most probably formed the nucleus of the Ṛgveda.

The eighth Maṇḍala resembles the Family Books in that the majority of the hymns (1-66) were composed by the Kaṇva family [the rest of the hymns (67-103) were composed by other families].

The first Maṇḍala, however, is unlike the above-mentioned Books because it consists of a large number of hymns (191) composed by a number of poets, none of whom composed more than 26 hymns. It is probably a later addition, although many individual hymns are no doubt quite old. There can be no doubt, however, that Maṇḍala ten contains hymns of later origin, judging from subject matter, grammatical structure, and the rather conscious symmetrical arrangement on the part of the redactors, who inserted 191 hymns in the Maṇḍala, thereby matching the number found in the first Maṇḍala.

The ninth Maṇḍala consists of hymns addressed to Soma Pavamāna, that is, the clarified sacrificial liquid. Because there are only four hymns addressed solely to Soma in the other Maṇḍalas, it is safe to assume that the hymns of the ninth Book were taken from the other Maṇḍalas, perhaps for ritual purposes.

The date of the Ṛgveda is impossible to determine with accuracy, particularly the chronology of the separate Maṇḍalas and hymns. The best estimate may be within the range of sometime between the thirteenth to eighteenth century B.C. for the oldest hymns, to around the ninth or tenth century B.C. for the most recent of the hymns.

The only recension of the RV that has come down to us is the one of the Śākala school (śākhā). Another recension of the RV was possessed by the Bāṣkala school, which from all accounts, differed only very slightly from the Śākala version. For a brief account of the Ṛgvedic schools, see Arthur A. Macdonell, A History of Sanskrit Literature, reprinted by Motilal Banarsidass, Delhi, India (1965), pp. 42-43.

The important editions of the Rgveda are as follows:

1. Aufrecht, Theodor, editor. Die Hymnen des Rigveda. Fourth edition. Two volumes. Wiesbaden: Otto Harrassowitz, 1968 [reprinted from the second edition of 1877].

2. Bandhu, Vishva, in collaboration with Bhīm Dev, Amar Nath, K.S. Rāmaswāmi Śāstri, and Pītāmbar Datta. Ṛgveda with the Padapāṭha and the available portions of the Bhāṣya-s by Skandasvāmin and Udgītha, the Vyākhyā by Veṅkaṭa-Mādhava and Mudgala's Vṛtti based on Sāyaṇa-bhāṣya. Hoshiapur: Vishveshvaranand

Vedic Research Institute, 1965 [Parts 1 and 7], 1963 [Parts 2 and 3], 1964 [Parts 4-6]. Vishveshvaranand Indological Series, nos. 19-25.

3. Müller, F. Max, editor. Rig-Veda-Sanhita, the sacred hymns of the Brahmans: tog. with the commentary of Sayanacharya. Six volumes. London, 1849 [Vol. I], 1854 [Vol. II], 1856 [Vol. III], 1862 [Vol. IV], 1872 [Vol. V], 1874 [Vol. VI].

The second edition of this work appeared under the title The Hymns of the Rig-Veda with Sāyaṇa's commentary, 2. ed. based on a collection of new mss. Four volumes, London, 1890-92. It has since been reprinted by the Chowkhamba Sanskrit Series Office (Varanasi) [Chowkhamba Sanskrit Series, vol. 99] in 1966.

4. Sonatakke, N.S. and C.G. Kashikar. Ṛgveda-Saṃhitā with the Commentary of Sāyaṇāchārya. Five Volumes. Poona: Vaidika Saṃśodhana Maṇḍala, 1933 [Vol. I], 1936 [Vol. II], 1941 [Vol. III], 1946 [Vol. IV], 1951 [Vol. V].

The most important translations (complete) are the following works:

1. Geldner, Karl Friedrich. Der Rig-Veda aus dem Sanskrit ins Deutsche übersetzt. Four volumes. Cambridge, Mass.: Harvard University Press, 1951 [vols. 1-3], 1957 [vol. 4]. Vol. 4 is entitled Namen-und Sachregister zur Übersetzung dazu Nachträge und Verbesserung aus dem Nachlass des Übersetzers by Johannes Nobel [Harvard Oriental Series, vols. 33-6].

Note: This work is being translated into English and will be appearing in print shortly.

2. Grassmann, Hermann. Rig-Veda. Two volumes. Leipzig: F.A. Brockhaus, 1876-77.

3. Griffith, Ralph T.H. The Hymns of the Ṛgveda. Fourth edition. Two volumes. Calcutta: The Chowkhamba Sanskrit Series Office, 1963 [reprint]. Chowkhamba Sanskrit Studies, vol. 35.

4. Ludwig, Alfred. Der Rigveda. Six volumes. Prag: Verlag von F. Tempsky, 1876 [vols. 1 and 2], 1878 [vol. 3], 1881 [vol. 4], 1883 [vol. 5], 1888 [vol. 6].

There are also many important translations of parts of the Ṛgveda. Among them are:

1. Bhave, S.S. The Soma-Hymns of the Ṛgveda. Three volumes. Baroda: Oriental Institute, 1957 [Part 1], 1960 [Part 2], 1962 [Part 3]. M.S. University of Baroda Research Series, nos. 3, 5, 6.

2. Bose, Abinash Chandra. Hymns from the Vedas. New York: Asia Publishing House, 1966.

3. Hillebrandt, Alfred. Lieder des Ṛgveda. Göttingen: Vandenhoeck and Ruprecht, 1913.

4. Kaegi, Adolf and Karl Geldner. Siebenzig Lieder des Rigveda. Tübingen: Verlag der H. Laup'schen Buchhandlung, 1875.

5. Lommel, Hermann. Gedichte des Rig-Veda. München-Planegg: Otto Wilhelm Barth-Verlag Gmblt, 1955.

6. Macdonell, Arthur Anthony. Hymns from the Rigveda. Calcutta-London, 1922 [Heritage Indological Series].

7. ________. A Vedic Reader for Students. Madras: Oxford University Press, 1960 [reprinted from the 1917 edition].

8. Müller, F. Max. Vedic Hymns. I. Hymns to the Maruts, Rudra, Vāyu, and Vāta. Delhi: Motilal Banarsidass, 1964 [reprinted from the Sacred Books of the East Series, vol. 32: originally published in 1891].

9. Oldenberg, Hermann. Vedic Hymns. II. Hymns to Agni (Maṇḍalas I-V). Delhi: Motilal Banarsidass, 1964 [reprinted from the Sacred Books of the East Series, vol. 46: originally published in 1897]. Also reprinted by Dover Publications (N.Y.) in 1963.

10. Renou, Louis. Études Védiques et Pāṇinéennes. Seventeen volumes. Paris: E. De Boccard, Éditeur, 1955 [vol. 1], 1956 [vol. 2], 1957

[vol. 3], 1958 [vol. 4], 1959 [vol. 5], 1960 [vol. 7], 1961 [vols. 8 and 9], 1962 (vol. 10], 1964 [vols. 12 and 13], 1965 [vol. 14], 1966 [vol. 15], 1967 [vol. 16], 1969 [vol. 17].

These volumes contain either translations, commentaries, or both. Volumes 6 and 11 have not been included because they deal with different topics. The above volumes are part of the Publications de l'Institut de Civilisation Indienne, fasc. 1, 2, 4, 6, 9, 12, 14, 16, 17, 20, 22, 23, 26, 27, 30. These numbers correspond to the volumes cited above in their respective order.

11. Thieme, Paul. Gedichte aus dem Rig-Veda. Stuttgart: Philipp Reclam Jun., 1964.

12. Velankar, H.D. "Hymns to Indra by the Viśvāmitras," Journal of the University of Bombay [Hereafter JUB] 3 (May 1935).

13. _______. "Hymns to Indra by the Vāmadevas," JUB 6 (May 1938).

14. _______. "Hymns to Indra by the Atris," JUB 8 (September 1939).

15. _______. "Hymns to Indra by the Gṛtsamadas," JUB 9 (September 1940).

16. _______. "Hymns to Indra by the Bhāradvājas," JUB 10-11 (September 1941-September 1942).

17. _______. "Family-Hymns in the Family-Maṇḍalas," Journal of the Bombay Branch of the Royal Asiatic Society 18 (1942).

18. _______. "Hymns to Indra by the Vāsiṣṭhas," JUB 13 (2), (September 1944).

19. _______. "Hymns to Indra in Maṇḍala VIII," JUB 15 (September 1946):1-28.

20. _______. "Hymns to Indra in Maṇḍala I," JUB 17 (September 1948):1-22.

21. _______. "Hymns to Indra in Maṇḍala I," JUB 18 (September 1949):6-25.

22. _______. "Hymns to Indra in Maṇḍala I," JUB 20 (September 1951):17-34.

23. _______. "Hymns to Indra in Maṇḍala X," JUB 21 (September 1952):1-20.

24. _______. "Hymns to Indra in Maṇḍala X," JUB 22 (September 1953):6-26.

25. _______. "Hymns to Indra in Maṇḍala X," JUB 23 (September 1954):1-18.

26. _______. "The Creation Hymns in ṚV X," Proceedings of the All India Oriental Conference (17th session), Ahmedabad, 1953, pp. 61-66.

27. _______. "Hymns to Agni in Maṇḍala VI," JUB 24 (September 1955):36-64.

28. _______. "Hymns to Agni in Maṇḍala VII," JUB 25 (September 1956):9-31.

29. _______. "Agni Hymns in Maṇḍala VIII," JUB 26 (September 1957):1-24.

30. _______. "Hymns to Agni in Maṇḍala X," JUB 27 (September 1958):1-28.

31. _______. Ṛgveda-Saṃhitā: Maṇḍala VII. Bombay: Bharatiya Vidya Bhavan, 1963 [Bharatiya Vidya Series 23].

32. _______. Ṛgveda Maṇḍala II. Bombay: University of Bombay, 1966.

33. _______. Ṛgveda Maṇḍala III. Bombay: University of Bombay, 1968.

Other titles of interest

1. Channa, Devraj. Ṛg-Bhāṣya-Sangraha. Delhi, 1961.

2. Datta, Manmatha Nāth. Rigveda Samhita (text with Sāyana's commentary and a literal prose English translation). Calcutta, 1907-13 [Wealth of India Series, 2. Ser. 1].

3. Kapali Sastry, T.V. Ṛgveda-Saṃhitā with Sanskrit Commentary, entitled Siddhāñjana. Pondicherry: Sri Aurobindo Ashram. [Vol. 1, Part 1 (RV 1. 1-32), 1950; Vol. I, Part 2 (RV I. 33-121), 1951].

4. Patankar, R.N. Vedabhāṣyasāra of Bhaṭṭoji Dīkṣita. Bombay, 1947 [Bhāratīya Vidyā Series 12].

5. Peterson, Peter. Hymns from the Ṛgveda. Edited by H.D. Velanker. Poona, 1959 [Bombay Sanskrit Series, 36; 7th edition, being a reprint of the 4th edition].

6. Raja, C. Kunhan. Ṛgvedavyākhyā Mādhavakṛtā. Madras: Adyar Library [Part I: Aṣṭaka I, adhyāyas 1-4, 1939: Adyar Library Series 22; Part II: aṣṭaka I, adhyāyas 5-8, 1947: Adyar Library Series 61].

7. ______. Ṛgveda-Bhāṣya of Skandasvāmin. Madras, 1935 [Madras University Sanskrit Series 8. This work comprises the first aṣṭaka].

8. ______. "Ṛgvedabhāṣya of Skandasvāmin (for 5th and 6th Maṇḍalas)," Adyar Library Bulletin (Brahmavidyā: Adyar) I (1937), XIV-XVI (1950-1952).

9. Sarup, Lakshman. Ṛgveda-Saṃhitā with Ṛgarthadīpikā of Veṅkaṭamādhava. Four volumes. Lahore: Motilal Banarasi Dass [for the first three volumes; n.d. available] and Banaras, 1955 [vol. 4; although two more volumes are projected, I have no information as to their existence].

10. Śāstrī, K. Sāmbaśiva and Ravi Varma. The Ṛk-Saṃhitā with the Bhāṣya of Skandasvāmin and Dīpikā of Veṅkaṭamādhavarya. Trivandrum, 1929 [Part I], 1933 [Part II], 1942 [Part III] [Trivandrum Sanskrit Series 96, 115, 142].

11. Satavalekar, S.D. Ṛgveda-Saṁhitā. Pardi: Svādhyāya Maṇḍala, 1957 [third edition].

12. Sharma, Aryendra and K. Sitaramaiya. Ṛgarthasāra of Dinakara Bhaṭṭa. Hyderabad, 1959 [Sanskrit Academy, Osmania University].

B. Sāmaveda-Saṃhitā 'The Collection of the Sāmaveda, i.e., the Knowledge of Chants (sā́man-).'

Three recensions of the Sāmaveda have come down to us: the Kauthuma, Rāṇāyanīya, and the Jaiminīya. The best known, the Kauthuma, consists of two parts: the Ārcika 'the strophe collection,' and the Uttarārcika 'the latter, subsequent, or second strophe collection.' The length of the Saṃhitā is 1810 verses. Of these 261 verses are repeated, and all but 75 are found in the Ṛgveda. The explanation of the close association between the Ṛg- and Sāma-veda Saṃhitā's is no doubt found in the performance of the sacrifice, although it is most probable that a portion of the Ṛgveda originated independently from the sacrificial ritual cycle. Regardless of this fact, the latter Collection was employed in connection with the other Saṃhitā's (i.e., the Sāma- and Yajur-vedas) by priests (brā́hmaṇas) who from antiquity possessed and performed rather complicated sacrificial rites: in particular, the Soma sacrifice. Some priestly families had as their main duty within the sacrificial ritual the recitation of the verses and strophes of the Ṛgveda. The priests within these families were called Hó̄tṛ's 'Invokers' or 'Offerers.' During the same ritual performance, sacrificial chants (sā́man's-) were also sung upon a strophe or ṛ́c-, and so many of the strophes were collected from the Ṛgveda to be inserted in the Collection (Saṃhitā-) of the Udgātṛ́ ('Singer'; 'Chanter') priest.

The Sāmaveda, as has been noted, is divided into two parts: the Ārcika and Uttarārcika. The first, the Ārcika, consists of 585 strophes (ṛ́c-) to which the various chants (sā́man-) belong. A strophe can be sung to various chants and vice versa. The Ārcika itself contains only the first strophe of each chant as an aid in recollecting the tune.

The Uttarārcika consists of 400 chants, mostly consisting of three strophes each (two contain as many as twelve strophes) out of which stotrá's (that is, a laud or chant consisting of a certain number of strophes which are put to melody) are sung at the chief sacrifices. Thus the Uttarārcika contains the complete text of the stanzas to be employed. The chants to the strophes of the Sāmaveda were taught orally, but in later times songbooks or Gānas were written to describe the chants. The titles of these songbooks are the Grāmageyagāna, Āraṇyagāna (or Āraṇyageyagāna), Ūhagāna, and Ūhyagāna.

The importance of the Sāmaveda lies in the sacrificial and magical spheres, for the chants were believed to possess 'magical' power. On this basis it is probably true that the original meaning of *sáman* is 'appeasing' or 'propitiatory song.'

The important editions of the *Sāmaveda* are:

1. Bhattacharya, B.B. *Sāmaveda-Saṃhitā with Sāyaṇa's Bhāṣya: Pūrvārcika*. Calcutta, 1936 [Calcutta Sanskrit Series XVI].

2. Caland, W. *Die Jaiminīya-Saṃhitā mit einer Einleitung über die Sāmaveda-literatur*. Breslau, 1907. [*Indische Forschungen*, 2].

3. Dīkṣita, Nārāyaṇa Svāmi. *Sāmaveda* (*Kauthumaśākhīya*). Aundh: Svādhyāya Maṇḍala, 1942.

4. Rāja, C. Kunhan. *Sāmaveda-Saṃhitā, with commentaries of Mādhava and Bharatasvāmin*. Madras: The Adyar Library, 1941 [The Adyar Library Series, no. 26].

5. Sāmaśramī, Satyavrata. *Sāma-Veda Saṃhitā. With the commentary of Sāyaṇa Āchārya*. Five volumes. Calcutta, 1871-78 [*Bibliotheca Indica*].

6. Satavalekar, S.D. *Sāmaveda-Saṁhitā*. Third edition. Pardī: Svādhyāya Mandala, 1956.

7. Stevenson, J. *Saṃhitā of the Sāma-Veda*. London, 1843. [the Rāṇāyaṇīya text].

8. Vira, Raghu. *Sāma-Veda of the Jaiminīyas*. Lahore, 1938. [Sarasvati Vihara Series, no. 3].

The translations of the Sāmaveda include the following:

1. Benfey, Th., *Sāmavedārcikam. Die Hymnen des Sāmaveda*. Leipzig, 1848 [reprinted in Darmstadt: Wissenschaftliche Buchgesellschaft, 1968. Two volumes].

2. Devi Chand. *Sāmaveda*. Hoshiarpur: All-India Dayananda Salvation Mission, 1963.

3. Dharmadeva. *Sāmaveda-Saṃhitā*. Jwalapur: Anand Kutir, 1967.

4. Griffith, Ralph T.H. The Hymns of the Sāmaveda. Fourth edition. Varanasi: Chowkhamba Sanskrit Series Office, 1963 [Chowkhamba Sanskrit Studies, vol. XXVIII. Reprint].

5. Stevenson, J. Translation of the Saṃhitā of the Sāma Veda. London, 1842 and Calcutta, 1906.

Other titles of interest:

1. Aiyar, T.K. Rajagopala. "The Music of the Samaveda Chants," Journal of the Music Academy (Madras) 20 (1949):144-151.

2. W. Caland. "Zur Frage über die Entstehung des Sāmaveda," Wiener Zeitschrift für die Kunde des Morgenlandes 22:436f.

3. Faddegon, B. Studies on the Sāmaveda, Part I. Amsterdam, 1951 [Verhandelingen der Koninklijke Akademie van Wetenschappen te Amsterdam. Afdeeling Letterkunde. Nieuwe Reeks. Deel 57, no. 1].

4. Hoogt, J.M. van der. The Vedic Chant Studied in its Textual and Melodic Form. Wageningen, 1929.

5. Iyer (Gayatonde), Shakuntala. "The Sāmans," JUB 31 (September 1962):35-61.

6. _______. "The Sāmans-II," JUB 32 (September 1963):89-126.

7. Raghavan, V. "Sāma Veda and Music," Journal of the Music Academy (Madras) 33 (1962):127-133.

8. Renou, Louis. "Études Védiques," Journal Asiatique 240 (1952):133-154.

9. _______. "List of words and forms in the Sāmaveda," Vāk 2 (December 1952):100-116.

10. J.F. Staal. Nambudiri Veda Recitation. 'S-Gravenhage: Mouton and Co., 1961 [Disputationes Rheno-Trajectinae, vol. V].

11. Albrecht Weber. "Über die Literatur des Sāmaveda," Indische Studien 1:25f.

C. Yajurveda-Saṃhitā 'The Collection of the Yajurveda, i.e., the knowledge of sacrificial formulae (yájus-).'

Quite properly the title should be the Saṃhitā's of the Yajurveda because of the number of schools which belong to it. The Yajurveda itself is separated into two main divisions: the White (śuklá-) Yajurveda and the Black (kṛṣṇá-) Yajurveda. The difference between these two works is that the White Yajurveda contains only the sacrificial formulae without any explanation as to their use in the ritual; the Black Yajurveda, on the other hand, does contain an explanation and discussion of the sacrificial rites to which the formulae belong. In other words, the Black Yajurveda possesses a Brāhmaṇa: a term which will be discussed in the second chapter. A further difference is that the White Yajurveda, unlike the Black Yajurveda, rarely pays any attention to the Hótṛ priest and his duties.

The reason why 'White' and 'Black' adjoin Yajurveda is not entirely clear. It is widely assumed that since the White Yajurveda consists only of sacrificial formulae and is separated from the explanatory matter found in the Brāhmaṇa's it is śuklá-'clear' or well-arranged, whereas the Black Yajurveda is just the opposite. M. Winternitz (A History of Indian Literature. Third edition. Calcutta: University of Calcutta, 1962, Vol. 1, Part 1, p. 149, n. 2), however, believes that the White Yajurveda owes its name to the sun, giving as possible proof the Śatapatha Brāhmaṇa 14.9.4, 33 (compare 4.4.5, 19) which contains the statement that the śuklā́ni yájūṃṣi 'white sacrificial formulae' are revealed by the sun and hence called ādityāni 'pertaining to the sun.' The Viṣṇu-Purāṇa 3.5 also relates that the Yājñavalkya received new sacrificial utterances from the sun.

The Yajurveda as a whole is the "prayer-book" for the Adhvaryú priest (the priest who carries out the manual duties of the sacrifice and who also recites the sacrificial prayers or yájus-). Because this priest had many separate sacrificial duties to perform, differences of opinion could easily arise with regard to the proper procedure, thus leading to the formation of special manuals and prayer-books. These manuals form what are now the difference recensions of the schools of the Yajurveda. Thus in the Black Yajurveda there are four Saṃhitā's and in the White Yajurveda one Saṃhitā having two recensions. The Black Yajurveda Saṃhitā's are closely interrelated, discussing the same subject matter in sometimes idential or nearly identical language. Their titles are as follows:

1. Kāṭhaka-Saṃhitā, the recension of the Kaṭha School;

2. Kapiṣṭhala-Kaṭha-Saṃhitā, the recension of the Kapiṣṭhala School;

3. Maitrāyaṇī-Saṃhitā, the recension of the Maitrāyaṇīya School;

4. Taittirīya-Saṃhitā, the recension of the Taittirīya School.

The White Yajurveda is called the Vājasaneyi-Saṃhitā, Vājasaneya being a patronymic meaning 'the son of Vājasani.' Two distinct versions have been handed down: one by the Kāṇva School and the other by the Mādhyaṃdina School. These two recensions agree almost entirely in content; the chief difference rests in variants of the sacrificial formulae.

One important feature of the Yajurveda is that it supplies the formulae for the entire sacrificial ceremonial, thus differing from the Sāmaveda (and to a lesser extent, the Ṛgveda) which deals only with the Soma sacrifice.

The important editions of the Yajurveda are:

Kāṭhaka-Samhita:

1. Satavalekar, S.D. Yajurvedīya Kāṭhaka Saṃhitā. Aundh: Svādhyāya Maṇḍala, 1943.

2. von Schroeder, Leopold. Kāṭhakam. Die Saṃhitā der Kaṭha-Śākhā. Three volumes. Leipzig: F.A. Brockhaus, 1900 [Vol. 1: reprinted in 1970 by Franz Steiner Verlag GMBH (Wiesbaden)], 1909 [vol. 2: reprinted in 1971 by same], 1910 [vol. 3: reprinted in 1972 by same].

Note: R. Simon has brought out an index of words to the von Schroeder edition under the title Index verborum zu L. v. Schroeder's Kāṭhakam-Ausgabe, Leipzig, 1912 [reprinted in 1972 by Franz Steiner Verlag].

Kapiṣṭhala-Kaṭha-Saṃhitā

1. Vira, Raghu. Kapiṣṭhala-Kaṭha-Saṃhitā. A Text of the Black Yajurveda. Delhi: Meharchand Lachhmandas, 1968 [reprinted from the 1932 edition].

Maitrāyaṇī-Saṃhitā

1. Satavalekar, S.D. Maitrāyaṇīya Saṁhitā Yajurvedīyā. Aundh: Svadhyaya Mandala, 1942.

2. von Schroeder, Leopold. Māitrayanī Saṃhitā. Die Samhita der Maitrāyaṇīya-Śākhā. Four volumes. Leipzig: F.A. Brockhaus, 1881 [Book I: reprinted in 1970 by Franz Steiner Verlag GMBH (Wiesbaden)] 1883 [Book II: reprinted in 1971 by the same], 1885 [Book III: reprinted in 1972 by the same], 1886 [Book IV: reprinted in 1972 by the same].

Taittirīya-Saṃhitā

1. Kṛṣṇayajurvedīya-Taittirīya-Saṃhitā. Śrīmat-Sāyaṇācārya-viracita-bhāṣya-sametā. Etat pustakaṃ Taḷekaro-'pāhva-Narahari-Śāstribhiḥ saṃśodhitam [for vols. 1-4; Kā° Ve° Śā° Saṃ° Kāśīnātha-Śāstrī Āgāśe ity etaiḥ saṃśodhitam: vols. 5-8]. Tac ca Rāvabahādūra ity upapada-dhāribhiḥ Gaṅgādhara Bāpūrāva Kāḷe. Puṇyākhya-pattane. Ānandāśrama-saṃskṛta-granthāvaliḥ. Granthāṅkah 42. Eight volumes 1959 [vol. 1], 1960 [vol. 2], 1961 [vol. 3], 1966 [vol. 4-7], 1959 [vol. 8].

2. Röer, E.B., E.B. Cowell, R.N. Vidyāratna, M.Ch. Nyāyaratna, S. Sāmaśramī. The Sanhitā of the Black Yajur Veda, with the commentary of Mādhava Āchārya. Six volumes. Calcutta, 1854-1899 [Bibliotheca Indica Series].

3. Weber, Albrecht. Die Taittirīya-Saṃhitā. Two volumes. Leipzig: F.A. Brockhaus, 1871-72.

Vājasaneyi-Saṃhitā

1. Bhaṭṭa, Ratnagopāla, and Mādhava Śāstrī. Kāṇvasaṃhitā. With Commentary of Sāyaṇa. Parts 1-3. Benaras; 1908-15.

2. Satavalekar, S.D. Śukla-Yajurvedīya Kāṇva-Saṁhitā. Aundh: Svādhyāya Maṇḍala, 1940.

3. ______. Vājasaneyi-Mādhyandina-Śukla-Yajurveda-Saṁhitā. Third edition. Pardi: Svādhyāya Maṇḍala, 1957.

4. Sukla Yajurveda-Samhita (Vajasaneyi-Madhyandina), with the Mantra-Bhashya of Mahamahopadhyaya-Srimad-Uvatacharya and the Veda-Dipa-Bhashya of Sriman-Mahidhara. Delhi: Motilal Banarsidass, 1971.

5. Weber, Albrecht. The Vājasaneyi-Sanhitā in the Mādhyandina-and the Kāṇva Śākhā. With the Commentary of Mahīdhara. Berlin: Ferd. Dummler's Verlagsbuch-handlung and London: Williams and Norgate. 1852 [The White Yajurveda, vol. 1]. Reprinted by Chowkhamba Sanskrit Series Office (Varanasi) [CSS,103], (?) 1966.

The translations of these works are the following:

1. Devi Chand, editor and translator. The Yajur Veda. New Delhi, 1965.

2. Griffith, Ralph T.H. The Texts of the White Yajurveda. Third edition. Banaras: Shri B.N. Yadav, Proprietor, E.J. Lazarus and Co., 1957 [reprint].

3. Keith, Arthur Berriedale. The Veda of the Black Yajus School entitled Taittirīya Sanhitā. Two volumes. Delhi: Motilal Banarsidass. 1967 [reprint from the 1914 edition. Harvard Oriental Series, vols. 18 and 19].

Note: There are no translations of the other three Black Yajurveda Samhita's.

D. Atharvaveda-Saṃhitā 'The Collection of the Atharaveda, i.e., the knowledge of the Atharvans or fire-priests' [compare Avestan Ātar 'Fire'].

The oldest name of the Atharvaveda is Atharvāñgirasaḥ, a designation found in the text itself. This compound is composed of Atharvan and Añgiras, both of which are names of two ancient families of priests. But it appears too that these two names possessed the meaning of '"magic" formulae.' Thus both referred not only to the priestly families but also to the magic formulae of these families. The Atharvan formulae were employed for healing purposes and thus were associated with 'holy' or 'white' magic, while the Añgiras formulae were employed as curses against enemies, rivals, etc. and thus associated with hostile or 'black' magic.

The Atharvaveda, unlike the other three Saṃhitā's, originally played no role in the major sacrifices. The chief purpose of this work was to appease, bless, and to curse. It thus represented a collection of texts which fitted the function of domestic priests who employed the hymns as imprecations against such diseases as jaundice, leprosy, blockage of the urinal tract, or against such evil beings as enemies, sorcerers, witches, demons, and noxious animals. On the more positive side the hymns were employed for the purpose of matrimonial happiness, for protection, fame, concord, virile power, superiority, the retention of sacred learning, for the purpose of gaining the love of a woman or man, luck in gambling, the birth of sons, to establish one in sovereignity, etc.

Quite apart from these are hymns which contain a relatively advanced philosophical content. The theosophical and cosmogonic speculations contained in these hymns are on the whole more advanced than the material found within the Ṛgveda and point more to the speculations of the Āraṇyakas and Upaniṣads.

Because of the contents of the Atharvaveda, a considerable time span elapsed before it attained to the rank of a canonical or orthodox work. Thus the phrase trayī vidyā 'threefold knowledge' was standard in the older works, referring to the Ṛg-, Sāma- and Yajur-veda's; the Atharvaveda was passed over or only mentioned after the trayī vidyā. The last Book (XX) of the Śaunaka recension, a late addition to the Atharvaveda, was undoubtedly added to establish a claim for the Collection to be the fourth Veda; its subject-matter is related to the Soma sacrifice and originates from the Ṛgveda.

The Atharvaveda possesses two recensions: the Śaunaka school and the Paippalāda school. The former is the standard and popular recension consisting of 731 hymns of about 6000 stanzas divided into 20 books. The latter recension was discovered in Kashmir by Georg Buhler in 1875 and has since been published (see below).

The important editions of the Atharvaveda are:

Śaunaka Atharvaveda

1. Bandhu, Vishva, in collaboration with Bhīmdev, Vidyānidhi and Munīshvar Dev. Atharvaveda (Śaunaka) with the Padapāṭha and Sāyaṇācārya's Commentary. Four volumes. Hoshiarpur: Vishveshvaranand Vedic Research Institute, 1960 [vol. 1], 1961 [vols. 2 and 3], 1962 [vol. 4].

2. Pandit, Shankar Pāndurang. Atharvaveda-Saṃhitā with the Commentary of Sāyaṇācārya. Four volumes. Bombay, 1895-98.

3. Roth, R. and W.D. Whitney. Atharva Veda Sanhitā. Third edition. Bonn: Ferd. Dümmlers Verlag, 1966 [reprinted from the second edition brought out by Max Lindenau, 1924].

4. Satavalekar, S.D. Atharvaveda-Saṁhitā. Aundh: Svādhyāya Maṇḍala, 1939 [second edition, 1943; third edition, 1957].

Paippalāda Atharvaveda

1. Barret, LeRoy Carr. "The Kashmirian Atharva Veda, Book One," Journal of the American Oriental Society [Hereafter JAOS] 26 (1905):197-295.

2. ______. ". . ., Book Two," JAOS 30 (1910:187-258.

3. ______. ". . ., Book Three," JAOS 32 (1912):343-90.

4. ______. ". . ., Book Four," JAOS 35 (1915):42-101.

5. ______. ". . ., Book Five," JAOS 37 (1917):257-308.

6. Edgerton, Franklin. "The Kashmirian Atharva Veda, Book Six," JAOS 34 (1914):374-411.

7. Barret, L.C. "The Kashmirian Atharva Veda, Book Seven," JAOS 40 (1920):145-69.

8. ______. ". . ., Book Eight," JAOS 41 (1921):264-89.

9. ______. ". . ., Book Nine," JAOS 42 (1922):105-46.

10. ______. ". . ., Book Ten," JAOS 43 (1923):96-115.

11. ______. ". . ., Book Eleven," JAOS 44 (1924):258-69.

12. ______. ". . ., Book Twelve," JAOS 46 (1926):34-48.

13. ______. ". . ., Book Thirteen," JAOS 48 (1928):34-65.

14. ______. ". . ., Book Fourteen," JAOS 47 (1927):238-49.

15. ______. ". . ., Book Fifteen," JAOS 50 (1930):43-73.

16. ______. . . ., Books Sixteen and Seventeen. New Haven: American Oriental Society, 1936 [American Oriental Series, vol. 9].

17. ______. ". . ., Book Eighteen," JAOS 58 (1938):571-614.

18. ______. . . ., Books Nineteen and Twenty. New Haven: American Oriental Society, 1940 [American Oriental Series, vol. 18].

19. Bhattacharya, Durgamohan. Atharvavedīya Paippalāda Saṃhitā. First Kāṇḍa. Calcutta, 1964 [Calcutta Sanskrit College Research Series, 26; Texts, 14].

21. ______. Atharvavedīya Paippalāda Saṃhitā. Volume 2. Calcutta, 1970 [CSCRS, 62; Texts, 20].

21. Vira, Raghu. Atharvaveda of the Paippalādas. Lahore: 1936 [Books 1-13: Sarasvatī Vihara Series, I], 1940 [Books 14-18: S.V. Series, IX], 1942 [Books 19-20, with indexes: S.V. Series, XII].

Complete translations of the *Śaunaka Atharvaveda* are:

1. Griffith, Ralph T.H. *The Hymns of the Atharvaveda*. Two volumes. Varanasi: The Chowkhamba Sanskrit Series Office, 1968 [Chowkhamba Sanskrit Studies, vol. 66. reprint].

2. Whitney, William Dwight. *Atharva-Veda Saṃhitā*. Edited by Charles Rockwell Lanman. Two volumes. Delhi: Motilal Banarsidass, 1962 [reprinted from the 1905 edition: Harvard Oriental Series, vols. 7-8]. Second Indian reprint edition: 1971.

Translations of parts of the *Śaunaka* text are:

1. Bloomfield, Maurice. *Hymns of the Atharva-Veda*. Delhi: Motilal Banarsidass, 1964 [reprinted from the 1897 edition. Sacred Books of the East Series, vol. 42]. This book has also been reprinted by Greenwood Press (N.Y.) in 1969.

2. Grill, Julius. *Hundert Lieder des Atharva-Veda.* Tübingen, 1879 [Second edition. Stuttgart: Verlag von W. Kohlhammer, 1888]. The second edition has since been reprinted by Dr. Martin Sändig oHG (Wiesbaden) in 1971.

3. Henry, V. *Atharva-Véda. Traduction et commentaire. Le livre VII*. Paris, 1892.

4. _______. *Atharva-Véda. Les livres VIII et IX*. Paris, 1894.

5. _______. *Atharva-Véda. Les Livres X, XI et XII*. Paris, 1896.

6. _______. *Les hymns Rohitas. Livre XIII de l'Atharva-Véda*. Paris, 1891.

7. Weber, Albrecht. "Erstes Buch des Atharvaveda," *Indische Studien* [Hereafter *IS*] 4:393f.

8. _______. "Zweites Buch der Atharva-Saṃhitā," *IS* 13:129f.

9. _______. "Drittes Buch der Atharva-Saṃhitā," *IS* 17:177f.

10. _______. "Viertes Buch der Atharva-Saṃhitā," *IS* 18:1f.

11. _______. "Fünftes Buch der Atharva-Saṃhitā," *IS* 18:154f.

# CHAPTER TWO

## BRĀHMAṆA'S

The term Brāhmaṇa (neuter) has the basic meaning of 'pertaining to, relating to, a bráhman-.' Bráhman- may refer to the fundamental, bearing, sustaining principle or power which may animate, cause to increase, etc.; or it may be applied to that class which we identify as priests, or more specifically, the repositories and communicators of sacred, sacrificial knowledge. Thus bráhmaṇa- may mean an explanation of, or speculation on that power we call bráhman-, the latter manifested as a mántra- 'sacred formula' or as any sacred knowledge which bears inherent fructifying power; or it may refer to an 'utterance or explanation of the bráhman- or repositor of sacred knowledge'. Used collectively bráhmaṇa- refers to the 'collection of these utterances and discussions of bráhman(s).' This latter explanation fits the definition of the Brāhmaṇa's as collective texts. These works are connected to the Saṃhitā's (principally the Ṛg-, Sāma-, and Yajur-vedas) in the sense that they connect the sacrificial mántra's with the sacrificial rite by explaining their direct mutual relation on the one hand, and on the other, their symbolical connection. In the former, they explain the particular ritual in its details; in the latter they explain the sacred significance of the ritual. It is under the latter heading that we find ancient legends, cosmogonic myths, linguistic and etymological explanations, and philosophic explanations cited in these works.

The differences among the Brāhmaṇa's of the several Saṃhitā's with regard to subject-matter consists in emphasizing the duties of the particular priest associated with that particular Saṃhitā. Thus the Brāhmaṇa's of the Ṛgveda specify the duties of the Hótṛ 'Invoker,' or 'Offerer," that priest who was responsible for reciting the ṛ́c's suitable for the sacrifice of the moment. The Brāhmaṇa's of the Sāmaveda confined themselves to the duties of the Udgātṛ́ the 'singer' or 'cantor' of the sāman's 'chants.' The Brāhmaṇa's of the Yajurveda concentrated on the duties of the Adhvaryú, the actual performer of the sacrifice, and the one who recites the yájus- or sacrificial prayers.

The date of the Brāhmaṇa's is roughly between 1000 B.C. to 700-650 B.C.

The Brāhmaṇa's of the various Saṃhitā's are listed as follows:

I. Brāhmaṇa's of the Ṛgveda

A. Aitareya Brāhmaṇa

This work consists of forty Adhyāya's or 'Lessons' divided in Pañcaka's 'Fifths.' The Brāhmaṇa is traditionally assigned to Mahidāsa Aitareya, who may have been the compiler or editor of the work. The subject-matter consists essentially of the Soma sacrifice called Agniṣṭoma (Adhyāyas 1-16) which lasts one day. It then deals with a Soma rite called Gavāmayana, a sattra (i.e., a sacrificial session lasting more than twelve days) lasting 360 days (Adhyāyas 17 and 18), then the 'Twelve Days' (Dvādaśāha) rite (Adhyāya's 19-24). Adhyāya's 25-32 deal with the Agnihotra or 'Fire Oblation,' and the final, supplementary portion (Adhyāya's 33-40) of the Aitareya deals with the consecration of the king and the position of his domestic priest or Purohita.

The important editions of the Aitareya Brāhmaṇa are:

1. Aufrecht, Th. Das Aitareya-Brāhmaṇa. Mit Auszügen aus dem Commentare von Sāyaṇācārya und anderen Beilagen. Bonn, 1879.

2. Bodas, M. Rajaram Shastri. The Aitareya Brahaman of the Rig Veda, carefully corrected by comparing with many mss. Bombay, 1895.

3. Haug, Martin, editor and translator. The Aitareya Brahmanam of the Rigveda. Two volumes. Bombay: Government Central Book Depot, 1863.

4. Aitareyabrāhmaṇam. Śrīmat-Sāyaṇācārya-viracita-bhāṣya-sameta. Etat pustakam Ka. Sā. Rā. Rā. Kāśīnātha Śāstrī Āgāśe ity etaiḥ saṃśodhitam. Puṇyākhya-pattana. Ānandāśrama-saṃskṛta-granthāvaliḥ. Granthāñkah 32. Two volumes [second edition], 1931.

5. Sāmaśramī, P.S. The Aitareya Brahmana of the Rig-Veda with Commentary of Sāyaṇa Ācārya. Four volumes. Calcutta, 1895-1906 [Bibliotheca Indica].

6. Pillai, P.K. Narayana. Aitareya Brāhmaṇa with the Vṛtti called Sukhāpradā, by Śrī Ṣaḍguruśiṣya. Trivandrum: [Trivandrum Sanskrit Series], 1942-1955. Volume I [Adhyāyas 1-15: 1942], Volume II [Adhyāyas 16-25: 1952], Volume III [Adhyāyas 26-32: 1955].

Note: I have no information on a fourth volume covering Adhyāyas 33-40.

The Brāhmaṇa has been translated by Haug [no. 3], and Arthur Berriedale Keith, Rigveda Brāhmaṇas: The Aitareya and Kauṣītaki Brāhmaṇas of the Rigveda. Cambridge, Mass.: Harvard University Press, 1920 [Harvard Oriental Series, vol. 25]. This work has since been reprinted by Motilal Banarsidass (Delhi) in 1971. Haug's translation has since been reprinted from the 1922 edition [Allahabad: Subhindra Nath Vasu at the Pāṇini Office, 1922] by the AMS Press in 1974 [Sacred Books of the Hindus, extra volume 4].

B. Kauṣītaki (Śāṅkhāyana) Brāhmaṇa

This Brāhmaṇa is closely related to the Aitareya Brāhmaṇa in subject matter. Thus Adhyāyas 7-30 deal with the Soma sacrifice; Adhyāya 2 discusses the Agnihotra and corresponds to Aitareya Brāhmaṇa 25. On the other hand, however, the subject matter in the Kauṣītaki is wider than the Aitareya. Thus the 'Setting Up of the Sacrificial Fire' [Agnyādhānam], the 'New and Full Moon Sacrifices' [Darśapūrṇamāsau], the 'Optional Sacrifices' [Kāmyā Iṣṭayaḥ], and the 'Four-Monthly Sacrifices' [Cāturmāsyāni] are discussed only in the Kauṣītaki. Although this Brāhmaṇa is not any longer than the Aitareya, it is uniform and methodical in its treatment of the subject matter, thereby giving justification to the view that the work is the product of one hand.

The work has been edited by B. Lindner [Das Kaushitaki Brāhmaṇa. Volume I: Text. Jena: Herman Costenoble, 1887] and translated by A.B. Keith [Rigveda Brāhmaṇas: see under Aitareya Brāhmaṇa]. A fairly recent edition of the work is the following: E.R. Sreekrishna Śarma, Kauṣītaki-Brāhmaṇa. Volume I (Text). Wiesbaden: Franz Steiner Verlag, 1968 [Verzeichnis der orientalischen Handschriften in Deutschland. Supplementband 9, 1].

## II. Brāhmaṇa's of the Sāmaveda

### A. Tāṇḍya Mahābrāhmaṇa [Pañcaviṃśa Brāhmaṇa, Prauḍha Brāhmaṇa]

The Sāmaveda possesses the greatest number of extant Brāhmaṇas, although there is a question whether a majority of these works are in reality Brāhmaṇas at all. In actuality only three works out of the nine or ten may be called Brāhmaṇas: the criterion being subject-matter. There are two major and independent schools of the Sāmaveda which possess Brāhmaṇas: the Tāṇḍins and Talavakāra or Jaiminīyas. The Brāhmaṇa of the Tāṇḍin school is called either the Tāṇḍya Mahābrāhmaṇa or Pañcaviṃśa Brāhmaṇa. Tāṇḍya is patronymic ('descendent of Taṇḍa' or 'belonging to the Tāṇḍin family'), to which mention is made of a ṛ́ṣi-(Vicakṣaṇa Tāṇḍya) in the Vaṃśa Brāhmaṇa 2.5-6 and to a teacher Tāṇḍya in Śatapatha Brāhmaṇa 6.1, 2, 25. In addition to these passages the Sāmavidhāna Brāhmaṇa 3.9, 3 makes mention of a teacher called Tāṇḍi(n). The second title, Pañcaviṃśa, means simply 'twenty-five' thus referring to the fact that this Brāhmaṇa consists of twenty-five chapters or books. Thus Tāṇḍya-Mahābrāhmaṇa may be translated as the 'Great Brāhmaṇa of Tāṇḍya' [Tāṇḍya may be considered the author or one of the authors of the work, a name also mentioned in Jaiminīya Brahmana 2.112] and Pañcaviṃśa Brāhmaṇa as the 'Brāhmaṇa of Twenty-Five (Chapters)'. A third name is also ascribed to this work: the Prauḍha Brāhmaṇa [Prauḍha = Mahā 'Great, Exalted'].

The contents of the Brāhmaṇa deal generally with the chants (sā́man's), lauds (stotrá's, that is, a chant of a certain number of ṛ́c's or strophes put to melody), and praises (stóma's, that is, the number of chanted verses either during a whole day of the Soma-sacrifice or during a part of it) of the various Soma sacrifices. Also mentioned are myths, legends, geographical information, and details relating to the Vrātya-Stoma's, or sacrifices by which Indians of Āryan origin not living according to the Brāhmaṇical system were admitted to this way of life.

The editions of the Pañcaviṃśa are:

1. Śāstrī, Pandit A. Chinnaswami and Pandit Pattābhirāma Śāstrī. The Tāṇḍyamahābrāhmaṇa Belonging to the Sāma Veda with the Commentary of Sāyaṇāchārya. Two volumes. Benares: Jai (Jaya) Krishnasas—Haridas Gupta, The Chowkhamba Sanskrit Series Office, 1935 [vol. 1] and 1936 [vol. 2], The Kashi Sanskrit Series (Haridās Sanskrit Granthamālā) no. 105 (Veda Section, no. 6).

2. Vedāntavāgīśa, Ānandachandra. Tāṇḍya Mahābrāhmaṇa with the Commentary of Sāyaṇa Āchārya. Two volumes. Calcutta, 1870, 1874 [Bibliotheca Indica Series].

The Brāhmaṇa has been translated by W. Caland, Pañcaviṃśa-Brāhmaṇa: The Brāhmaṇa of Twenty Five Chapters. Calcutta: Asiatic Society of Bengal, 1931 [Bibliotheca Indica Series].

A work of major interest with regard to this Brāhmaṇa is by E. W. Hopkins, "Gods and Saints of the Great Brāhmaṇa," Transactions of the Connecticut Academy of Arts and Sciences 15 (July 1909):23-69.

B. The Ṣaḍviṃśa Brāhmaṇa

As the name implies [ṣaḍviṃśa 'twenty-six(th)'] this Brāhmaṇa serves as a supplement to the Pañcaviṃśa Brāhmaṇa. It belongs to the Kauthuma school and deals mainly with the ceremonies and rituals related to the Soma sacrifices. The work consists of six chapters; the sixth chapter, however, seems to have been added to the work at a later time, and is called the Adbhuta Brāhmaṇa, a work which is sometimes treated as a separate Brāhmaṇa.

The editions of the Ṣaḍviṃśa Brāhmaṇa are:

1. Eelsingh, H.F. Ṣaḍviṃśabrāhmaṇam. Vijñāpanabhāṣyasahitam. Het Ṣaḍviṃśa-brāhmaṇa van de Sāmaveda, uitgegeven met een inleiding, de op naam van Sāyaṇa staande commentaar en aanteekeningen. Leiden, 1908 [Dissertation: Utrecht].

2. Sharma, Bellikoth Ramachandra. Ṣaḍviṃśa Brāhmaṇa with Vedārthaprakāśa of Sāyaṇa. Tirupati: Kendriya Sanskrit Vidyapeetha, 1967 [Kendriya Sanskrit Vidyapeetha Series no. 9].

The work has been translated by W.B. Bollee. Ṣaḍviṃśa-Brāhmaṇa. Utrecht: Drukkerij A. Storm, 1956. An analysis of the contents of the Ṣaḍviṃśa appeared in the Śaradāpīṭhapatrikā (Dwarka), 11 (August 1971):31f, under the title "Ṣaḍviṃśa-Brāhmaṇa: A Study" by K.S. Shukla.

C. Adbhuta Brāhmaṇa

This work comprises the sixth Adhyāya [of the Sharma edition; the fifth Adhyāya of the Eelsingh edition] of the Ṣaḍviṃśa Brāhmaṇa. As the name implies the Brāhmaṇa [adbhuta 'portent, omens'] deals with the appeasement of portents [adbhuta-śānti: Sayana in his introduction to the work].

The Adbhuta is included in the editions and translation of the Ṣaḍviṃśa Brāhmaṇa cited above. It has also been edited and translated by A. Weber (Zwei Vedische Texte über Omina und Portenta. Published in the Abhandlungen der Berliner Akademie der Wissenschaften, Philolhistor. klass, 1858). For a discussion of the Adbhuta Brāhmaṇa see N. Tsuji, "on the formation of the Adbhuta-Brāhmaṇa," Annals of the Bhandarkar Oriental Research Institute (Poona), 48-49 (1968):173-178.

D. Jaiminīya Brāhmaṇa

This text is the largest of the Sāmaveda Brāhmaṇas and perhaps the most important of all the Brāhmaṇas with reference to mythological and legendary material.

In general the Jaiminīya Brāhmaṇa parallels that of the Pañcaviṃśa Brāhmaṇa in subject-matter. Thus the Agniṣṭoma sacrifice is mentioned [Jaiminīya Brāhmaṇa 1.66-364; corresponds to Pañcaviṃśa Brāhmaṇa 6-9] as well as the Gavāmayana [JB 2.1-80; PB 4-5], the one day Soma sacrifices [Ekāha's: JB 2.81-234; PB 16-19], the Ahīna's [sacrifices lasting up to twelve days: JB 2.235-333; PB 20-22], the Sattras [sacrificial sessions lasting more than twelve days: JB 2.334-370; PB 23-25], and the twelve day rites [Dvādaśāha: JB 3; PB 10-15]. The Jaiminīya Brāhmaṇa, however, discusses the Agnihotra sacrifice [1.1-65] whereas the Pañcaviṃśa does not. But the Pañcaviṃśa possesses the yajussaṃhitā 'collection of sacrificial formulae' in the first chapter which was probably composed at a later date than the Brāhmaṇa proper, and the Viṣṭuti section (Chapters 2-3) which describe the manner in which the various stoma's are to be formed. A viṣṭuti- is a particular arrangement of verses which consists of three sections or rounds (paryāya's) each of which should contain each stanza in different or equal numbers. The treatment of these viṣṭuti's is not found in the Jaiminīya Brāhmaṇa.

Strictly speaking, it appears that the Jaiminīya Brāhmaṇa contains five chapters (Kāṇḍa's), the first three chapters of which have been discussed above and form the nucleus of the work. Chapter Four is styled the *Jaiminīya-Upaniṣad-Brāhmaṇa* or simply *Upaniṣad Brāhmaṇa*, a work which has been published separately and is actually an *Āraṇyaka*. Chapter Five consists of the *Ārṣeya Brahmana*, according to Macdonell [*A History of Sanskrit Literature*, p. 177], based no doubt on the fact that a Jaiminiya recension exists. It would be better, however, to treat the *Ārṣeya* as a separate work.

The only complete edition of the *Jaiminīya Brāhmaṇa* [*Kāṇḍa's* 1-3] is by Raghu Vira [*Jaiminīya Brāhmaṇa of the Sāmaveda*. Lahore: Sarasvati Vihara Series 2, 1937; republished in 1954 by Dr. Lokesh Chandra (co-editor), Nagpur: Sarasvati Vihara Series 31].

Lokesh Chandra has also published a separate work on the *Gavāmayana* section of the *Jaiminīya Brāhmaṇa*, entitled *Jaiminiya Brahmana of the Samaveda II, 1-80 (Gavamayana)* (Nagpur: Shri Lokesh Chandra, 1950 [Sarasvati Vihara Series, vol. 21].

The following works are partial editions and translations of the *Jaiminīya Brāhmaṇa*:

1. Bodewitz, H.W. *Jaiminiya Brahmana I.1-65.* Translation and commentary. Leiden: E.J. Brill, 1973 [Orientalia Rheno-Traiectina, vol. 17].

2. Caland, W. *Das Jaiminīya-Brāhmaṇa in Auswahl.* Amsterdam: Johannes Müller, 1919 [Verhandelingen der Koninklijke Akademie van Wetenschappen te Amsterdam. Afdeeling Letterkunde. Deel 1. Nieuwe Reeks, Deel LXI, no. 4]. Reprinted by Dr. Martin Sändig oHG (Wiesbaden) in 1970.

3. Hoffmann, Karl. "Textkritisches zum Jaiminīya-Brāhmaṇa," *Indo-Iranian Journal* (Hague) 4:1-36.

4. ______. "Die Weltentstehung nach dem Jaiminīya-Brāhmaṇa," *Münchener Studien zur Sprachwissenschaft* 27 (1970):59-67.

5. Kuiper, F.B.J. "Textcritical Notes on the *Jaiminīya Brāhmaṇa*," in *Mélanges d'indianisme à la mémoire de Louis Renou*. Paris: E. de Boccard, 1968 [Publications de l'Institut de Civilisation Indienne, 28], pp. 427-431.

6. Oertel, Hanns. "Extracts from the *Jaiminīya-Brāhmaṇa* and *Upaniṣad-Brāhmaṇa*," *JAOS* 15 (1892): 233-251.

7. _______. "Contributions from the Jaiminīya to the history of the Brāhmaṇa literature: First Series," JAOS 18 (1897):15-48.

8. _______. "Contributions . . .: Second Series," JAOS 19 (1898):97-125.

9. _______. "The Jaiminiya Brahmana Version of the Dirghajihvi Legend" [= Third Series of the "Contributions . . ."] International Congress of Orientalists, Third Series. Paris, 1897, pp. 225-239.

10. _______. "Contributions . . .: Fourth Series," JAOS 23 (1902):325-349 [only Sanskrit passages cited from the Jaiminīya and Śāṭyāyana Brāhmaṇa's].

11. _______. "Contributions . . .: Fifth Series," JAOS 26 (1905):176-196. "Additions to the Fifth Series of Contributions from the Jāiminiya Brāhmaṇa" (JAOS 26:176f.), JAOS 26:306-314.

12. _______. "Contributions . . .: Sixth Series," JAOS 28 (1907):81-98.

13. _______. "Contributions . . .: Seventh Series," Connecticut Academy of Arts and Sciences, Transactions 15 (1909):155-216.

14. _______. "Volkstümliche Erzahlungsmotiv in Jaiminīya-brāhmaṇa," Zeitschrift für Vergleichende Sprachforschung 69:26-28.

15. Viru, Raghu and Lokesh Chandra, "Studies in Jaiminīya-Brāhmaṇa: Book I," Acta Orientalia (Leiden) 22:55-74. [Also in Studia Indologica: Festschrift für Willibald Kirfel, Bonn: Selbstverlag des Orientalischen Seminars der Universität, 1955, pp. 255-276].

E. Sāmavidhāna Brāhmaṇa

This Brāhmaṇa was composed, as we learn from Sāyaṇa's commentary entitled the Vedārthaprakāśa [Introduction], for the purpose of achieving those ends (such as gaining heaven, warding off evils, etc.) ordinarily obtained through the great sacrifices (such as the Agnihotra, Agnyādhāna) by means of the proper arrangement of the sāman's. The reason for this substitute was due to eligibility. Only those with the means, as well as the mental and physical equipment and station could perform the great sacrifices. Thus the Brāhmaṇa was composed for those ineligible persons who desired to obtain the same ends. Through the proper 'arrangement of the Sāmans' (Sāmavidhāna), these ends could be achieved.

The editions and translations of this Brāhmaṇa are:

1. Burnell, A.C. The Sāmavidhāna-Brāhmaṇa (being the third Brāhmaṇa of the Sāmaveda). London, 1873 [text and English translation].

2. Konow, St. Das Sāmavidhānabrāhmaṇa, ein altindisches Handbuch der Zauberei. Halle, 1893 [text and German translation].

3. Sāmaśramī, S. "Sāmavidhāna Brāhmaṇa," Uṣā (Calcutta), vol. II (1895).

4. Sharma, B.R., editor. Sāmavidhāna Brāhmaṇa: with Vedārthaprakāśa of Sāyaṇa and Padārthamātra-vivṛti of Bharatasvāmin. Tirupati: Kendrīya Sanskrit Vidyapeetha, 1964 [Kendriya Sanskrit Vidyapeetha Series, no. 1].

F. Ārṣeya Brāhmaṇa

The Ārṣeya Brāhmaṇa consists of a list of the names of the sāman's occurring in the Grāmageyagāna and Āraṇyagāna. The Ūha- and Ūhya-gāna's, both of which are based upon the Uttarārcika, are omitted. As such this book is nothing but an anukramaṇikā, that is, an index or table of contents ('enumeration'). Although the title Ārṣeya ['relating to a ṛ́ṣi-'] suggests that the ṛ́ṣi's or ṛ́ṣi-singers are listed and discussed, this is not the case. However, the names of the chants are often suggestive of the names of the ṛ́ṣi's who composed them.

Each of the Sāmaveda schools (Kauthuma-Rāṇāyanīya and Jaiminīya) possessed their own recension of the work.

The editions of the Ārṣeya Brāhmaṇa are the following:

1. Burnell, A.C. The Ārṣeyabrāhmaṇa (being the fourth Brāhmaṇa of the Sāmaveda). Mangalore, 1876.

2. _______. The Jaiminīya text of the Ārṣeyabrāhmaṇa of the Sāmaveda. Mangalore, 1878.

3. Mādhavadāśa, Sāṅkhyatīrtha. Ārṣeya Brāhmaṇam. Calcutta: Śrī Bhāratī Publishing Co., n.d. [Devanāgarī text with Bengālī translation].

4. Sāmaśramī, Satyavrata. "Ārṣeya Brāhmaṇa with the commentary of Sāyaṇa." Uṣā (Calcutta), I (1891-1892). [This is the second edition of the work which came out originally in 1874].

5. Sharma, Bellikoth Ramachandra. Ārṣeya Brāhmaṇa with Vedārthaprakāśa of Sāyaṇa. Tirupati: Kendriya Sanskrit Vidyapeetha, 1967 [Kendriya Sanskrit Vidyapeetha Series, no. 8].

6. ______. Jaiminīya Ārṣeya-Jaiminīya Upaniṣad Brāhmaṇas. Tirupati: Kendriya Sanskrit Vidyapeetha, 1967 [Kendriya Sanskrit Vidyapeetha Series, nos. 5-6].

There is no English translation of the Ārṣeya Brāhmaṇa available to my knowledge.

G. Devatādhyāya Brāhmaṇa

This work deals with the divinities to which the sáman's are addressed, the etymology of the meters (chándas-) and their colors (várṇa-: 2.1). The term Devatādhyāya ('Lesson on the divinities') refers to the subject matter found primarily in Khaṇḍa 1.

The editions of this work are:

1. Burnell, A.C. The Devatādhyāyabrāhmaṇa (being the fifth Brāhmaṇa of the Sāmaveda). Mangalore, 1873.

2. Dikshitar, M. Ramanatha. Devatādhyāya Brāhmaṇa and Saṃhitopaniṣad. Mylapore, Madras, 1959.

3. Sāmaśramī, Satyavrata. Devatādhyāya Brāhmaṇa with the commentary of Sāyaṇa and a running commentary to the text in Bengali. Calcutta, 1875.

4. Sharma, Bellikoth Ramachandra. Devatādhyāya-Saṃhitopaniṣad-Vaṃśa-Brāhmaṇas with Commentaries. Tirupati: Kendriya Sanskrit Vidyapeetha, 1965 [Kendriya Sanskrit Vidyapeetha Series, nos. 2-4].

H. Mantra Brāhmaṇa

The title of this Brāhmaṇa may cause some confusion since it is part of a work called either the Upaniṣad Brāhmaṇa or Chāndogya Brāhmaṇa. The Mantra Brāhmaṇa comprises the first two chapters of prapāṭhaka's ('recitations'). The remaining eight prapāṭhaka's of the Upaniṣad or Chāndogya Brahmana are the Chāndogya Upaniṣad. The Mantra ('sacred speech,' 'sacred text being equated either to a ṛ́c- or sā́man-, or yájus-') Brāhmaṇa deals with the mántra's for the household (gṛ́hya) rites such as the birth and marriage rites.

The editions of the Mantra Brāhmaṇa are:

1. Bhattacharyya, Purgamohan. Chāndogya-Brāhmaṇa with the Commentaries of Guṇaviṣṇu and Sāyaṇa. Calcutta, 1958. [Calcutta Sanskrit College Research Series--Texts, No. 1].

2. Sāmaśramī, Satyavrata. Mantra Brāhmaṇa with a commentary and Bengālī translation. Serampore, 1872; Calcutta, 1873.

The first prapāṭhaka has been edited and translated into German by H. Stönner [Das Mantrabrāhmaṇa. I. Prapāṭhaka. Halle, 1901]. The second prapāṭhaka has been edited and translated into German by H. Jörgensen [Das Mantrabrāhmaṇa. 2. Prapāṭhaka. Darmstadt, 1911].

I. Saṃhitā-Upaniṣad Brāhmaṇa

This work deals with the secret meaning (upaniṣad-) of the saṃhitā, a word which is used in this work in the sense of a sāma-gāna or verse-chant which consists of melodizing with the use of the saptasvara's ['the seven notes on the musical scale usually consisting of niṣāda, ṛṣabha, gāndhāra, ṣaḍja, madhyama, dhaivata, pañcama: i.e., notes resembling the sound or pitch of an elephant, bull, goat, peacock, curlew or heron, horse, and koïl], are tuned in harmony and continuity [Sharma, op. cit., p. 20 under no. 4 of section G]. Besides treating the saṃhitā's, this Brāhmaṇa discusses the rewards of the chanter of saṃhitā's, the scientific aspects of melodization of sā́man's in different svára's in harmony and elaborated with the stobha [interjections occurring in sāman's] etc., and the dákṣiṇā's or sacrificial gifts given to the teacher upon the completion of one's education.

The editions of this work are:

1. Burnell, A.C. The Saṃhitopaniṣadbrāhmaṇa (being the seventh Brāhmaṇa of the Sāmaveda). Mangalore, 1877.

2. Dikshitar, M.R. [see no. 2 of section G].

3. Sharma, B.R. [see no. 4 of section G].

## J. Vaṃśa Brāhmaṇa

The Vaṃśa ('lineage') Brāhmaṇa is a short work dealing with the lineage of all the ṛṣi's, real and legendary, involved in the learning and tradition of the Sāmaveda.

The editions of this work include:

1. Burnell, A.C. The Vaṃśabrāhmaṇa (being the eighth Brāhmaṇa of the Sāmaveda). Mangalore, 1873.
2. Sāmaśramī, Satyavrata. "Vaṃśabrāhmaṇa" (with the Commentary of Sāyaṇa and Bengālī translation). Uṣā II (1892).
3. Sharma, B.R. [see no. 4 of section G].
4. Weber, A. "Das Vaṃśabrāhmaṇa des Sāmaveda" IS, Vol. IV, pp. 371f.

Note 1: The traditional listing of the Sāmaveda Brāhmaṇa's has been given by the commentator Sāyaṇa in his work Vedārthaprakāśa. The order of the eight works mentioned are as follows:

a. Prauḍha Brāhmaṇa

b. Ṣaḍviṃśa Brāhmaṇa

c. Sāmavidhāna (Sāmavidhi) Brāhmaṇa

d. Ārṣeya Brāhmaṇa

e. Devatādhyāya Brāhmaṇa

f. Upaniṣad Brāhmaṇa

g. Saṃhitopaniṣad Brāhmaṇa

h. Vaṃśa Brahmana

This list appears in the introductory verses (nos. 6-7) of his commentary. The fact that the Adbhuta Brāhmaṇa is not mentioned is understandable since it is found attached to the Ṣaḍviṃśa Brāhmaṇa in the manuscripts, but omission of the Jaiminīya Brāhmaṇa presents us with a real problem. Oertel [no. 9 of section D, pp. 225-226] writes the following:

"Considering its bulk and the number of legends contained in it, it is a strange fact that the Jaiminīya Brāhmaṇa is almost unknown to the ancillary literature of the Veda. . . . If it is thus established that Sāyaṇa knew the Jaiminīya Brāhmaṇa [this is established from the quotation of a passage appearing in the Jaiminīya B. in his own commentary on the Aitareya Brāhmaṇa (2.22)], why does he quote it so little? The explanation may perhaps be found in the close connection of, and the similarity between, the Jaiminīya and the Śāṭyāyana Brāhmaṇas. . . ."

The eight works listed by Sāyaṇa as being Brāhmaṇa's of the Sāmaveda are all connected to the Kauthuma and/or Rāṇāyanīya Schools. It is conceivable that this school was considered to be the more authentic in the Sāmaveda tradition by Sāyaṇa. It is also possible to assume that this school was the more active or even the only active school in Sāyaṇa's time and sphere of activity [south India].

Note 2: It is B.R. Sharma's contention [no. 4 of Section G and no. 5 of Section F] that the eight Brāhmaṇa's mentioned above were actually eight books of a single Brāhmaṇa known as Mahā- or Prauḍha-Brāhmaṇa. He believes that the title Mahā or Prauḍha-Brāhmaṇa does not fit well with the Pañcaviṃsa Brāhmaṇa alone. Therefore it seems likely that these eight books were written separately for the convenience of the priests and chandogá's or 'chanters of meters' [p. 9 of no. 4 of section G; and pp. 10-11 of no. 5 of section F].

Note 3: There existed a third major school which produced a Sāmaveda Brāhmaṇa, that of the Śāṭyāyana's. Evidence of the Brāhmaṇa is gleaned mainly from quotations found in Sāyaṇa's commentary to the Ṛgveda. The collection of passages from the Śāṭyāyana Brāhmaṇa fragments are found in Oertel [no. 7 of section D]. One may also consult T.R. Chintamani ["The Śāṭyāyana Brāhmaṇa." Journal of Oriental Research (Madras), vol. 5 (1931)] and Batakrishna Ghosh [Collection of the Fragments of lost Brāhmaṇas. Calcutta: Modern Publishing Syndicate, 1935].

## III. Brāhmaṇa's of the Yajurveda

### A. Taittirīya Brāhmaṇa

The Taittirīya Brāhmaṇa belongs to, and is, a continuation of the Taittirīya Saṃhitā of the Kṛṣṇa Yajurveda. This is, in fact, the only complete and independent Brāhmaṇa found within the Kṛṣṇa Yajurveda. This independent status may have been brought about by the desire of the Taittirīya school to emulate the Ṛgvedic tradition of Brāhmaṇa and Saṃhitā, a desire which led to the separation of both in the Vājasaneyi redaction as well [Keith, The Veda of the Black Yajus School entitled Taittirīya Sanhitā, I, p. lxxvi; for the Vājasaneyi redaction see section B below].

Among the subjects included in the Brāhmaṇa are explanations of the Rājasūya (1.6.1-8,10), the Agnihotra (2.1.1-11), and the list of victims for the human sacrifice (Puruṣamedha: 3.4.1-19). [See Dumont's articles below].

Among the editions of the Taittirīya Brāhmaṇa are:

1. Kṛṣṇayajurvedīyaṃ Taittirīyabrāhmaṇam. Śrīmat-Sāyaṇācārya-viracita-bhāṣya-sametam. Etat pustakaṃ Puṇyapattana-nivāsibhiḥ Goḍabole ity upāhvaiḥ Ve. Śā. Saṃ. Nārāyaṇa-Śāstribhiḥ saṃśodhitam, Puṇyākhya-pattane. Ānandāśrama-saṃskṛta-granthāvaliḥ. Granthāṅkaḥ 37. Three volumes, 1898 [second edition, 1934-38].

2. Mitra, Rājendralāla. The Taittirīya Brāhmaṇa of the Black Yajur Veda with the Commentary of Sāyaṇāchārya. Three volumes. Calcutta: Asiatic Society of Bengal, 1859 [vol. 1], 1862 [vol. 2], 1890 [vol. 3].

3. Sastri, A. Mahadeva and L. Srinivasacharya. The Taittiriya Brahmana with the Commentary of Bhattabhaskaramisra. Three volumes. Mysore, 1908-1913.

Paul Emile Dumont has edited and translated a large part of the Brāhmaṇa in the Proceedings of the American Philosophical Society [Hereafter PAPS]. The separate titles are as follows:

1. "The Horse-Sacrifice in the Taittirīya-Brāhmaṇa: The Eighth and Ninth Prapāṭhakas of the Third Kāṇḍa of the Taittirīya-Brāhmaṇa with Translation," PAPS 92 (1948):447-503.

2. "The Special Kinds of Agnicayana (or Special Methods of Building the Fire-Altar) According to the Kaṭhas in the Taittirīya-Brāhmaṇa: The Tenth, Eleventh, and Twelfth Prapāṭhakas of the Third Kāṇḍa of the Taittirīya-Brāhmaṇa with Translation," PAPS 95 (1951):628-675.

3. "The Iṣṭis to the Nakṣatras (or Oblations to the Lunar Mansions) in the Taittirīya-Brāhmaṇa: The First Prapāṭhaka of the Third Kāṇḍa of the Taittirīya-Brāhmaṇa with Translation," PAPS 98 (1954):204-223.

4. "The Full-Moon and New-Moon Sacrifices in the Taittirīya-Brāhmaṇa (First Part): The Second Prapāṭhaka of the Third Kāṇḍa of the Taittirīya-Brāhmaṇa with Translation," PAPS 101 (1957):216-243.

5. ". . . (Second Part): The Third Prapāṭhaka of the Third Kāṇḍa of the Taittirīya-Brāhmaṇa with Translation," PAPS 103 (1959):584-608.

6. ". . . (Third Part): The Part of the Hotar in the Full-Moon and New-Moon Sacrifices. The Fifth Prapāṭhaka of the Third Kāṇḍa of the Taittirīya-Brāhmaṇa with Translation," PAPS 104 (1960):1-10.

7. ". . . (Fourth Part): The Anuvākas 1-6 and 11 of the Seventh Prapāṭhaka of the Third Kāṇḍa of the Taittirīya-Brāhmaṇa with Translation," PAPS 105 (1961):11-36.

8. "The Animal Sacrifice in the Taittirīya-Brāhmaṇa: The Part of the Hotar and the Part of the Maitrāvaruṇa in the Animal Sacrifice: The Sixth Prapāṭhaka of the Third Kāṇḍa of the Taittirīya-Brāhmaṇa with Translation," PAPS 106 (1962):246-263.

9. "The Human Sacrifice in the Taittirīya-Brāhmaṇa: The Fourth Prapāṭhaka of the Third Kāṇḍa of the Taittirīya-Brāhmaṇa with Translation," PAPS 107 (1963):177-182.

10. "Taittirīya-Brāhmaṇa 3.7.7-10 and 3.7.12-14: Seven Anuvākas of the Seventh Prapāṭhaka of the Third Kāṇḍa of the Taittirīya-Brāhmaṇa with Translation," PAPS 107 (1963):446-460.

11. "The Agnihotra (or Fire-God Oblation) in the Taittirīya-Brāhmaṇa: The First Prapāṭhaka of the Second Kāṇḍa of the Taittirīya-Brāhmaṇa with Translation," PAPS 108 (1964): 337-353.

12. "The Kaukilī-Sautrāmaṇī in the Taittirīya-Brāhmaṇa: The Sixth Prapāṭhaka of the Second Kāṇḍa of the Taittirīya-Brāhmaṇa with Translation," PAPS 109 (1965):309-341.

13. "The Kāmya Animal Sacrifices in the Taittirīya-Brāhmaṇa: The Eighth Prapāṭhaka of the Third Kāṇḍa of the Taittirīya-Brāhmaṇa with Translation," PAPS 113 (1969):34-66.

The first three Prapāṭhakas of the first Kāṇḍa (the Ādhāna and Punarādhāna sections) have been edited and translated under the authority of the Mīmāṃsā Grantha Prakāśaka-Samiti of Poona under the title Kṛṣṇa-Yajurveda, new edition, Part I (containing Ādhāna and Punarādhāna sections) edited by Paṇḍit Vāmanśāstrī Kinjavadekar and English translation by S.M. Katre (Poona, 1938).

Note: In 1943 an edition of extracts from a lost Brāhmaṇa of the Kaṭha School was published by Meherchand Lachhman Dass (Lahore). The title of the work is Kāṭhaka-Brāhmaṇa-Saṃkalana and is edited by Suryakanta.

## B. Śatapatha Brāhmaṇa

Attached to the Vājasaneyi Saṃhitā is the 'Brāhmaṇa of a Hundred Paths' (Śata-patha), so called because it consists of one hundred Adhyāya's or 'Lessons.' Together with the Jaiminīya Brāhmaṇa this work must be ranked as the most important Brāhmaṇa, as far as the extensiveness of its subject-matter is concerned.

Like the Vājasaneyi Saṃhitā the Brāhmaṇa possesses two recensions: that of the Kāṇva School and that of the Mādhyaṃdina School. As far as the bulk of the work is concerned, a fair indicator would be the number of divisions. The Mādhyaṃdina recension consists of 14

Kāṇḍa's ('books' or 'divisions'), subdivided into 100 Adhyāyas, 438 Brāhmaṇa's, and 7,624 Kāṇḍika's. The Kāṇva recension consists of 17 Kāṇḍa's (the first, fifth, and fourteenth books being divided into two parts); its overall length is approximately the same as the Mādhyaṃdina recension.

As far as subject-matter is concerned the Brāhmaṇa discusses the Darśapūrṇamāsa Iṣṭi, the Agnādhāna, Agnihotra, Piṇḍapitṛyajña, Āgrāyaṇa Iṣṭi [Offering of the First-Fruits], Dākṣāyaṇa, Cāturmāsyāni, the Soma sacrifices, Vājapeya, Rājasūya, Abhiṣecanīya, Daśapeya, Keśavapanīya, Sautrāmaṇī, Agnicayana, the Sattra's, Aśvamedha, Puruṣamedha, Sarvamedha, funeral ceremonies, and the Pravargya sacrifices.

Needless to say this Brāhmaṇa contains many myths and legends of importance. Among them is the occurrence of a flood myth (1.8.1f.), the story of Purūravas and Urvaśī (11.5.1f.), and in the closing portion of the Śatapatha perhaps the crowning achievement of Vedic literature: the Bṛhad-Āraṇyaka-Upaniṣad.

The important editions of the Śatapatha in the Mādhyaṃdina recension are as follows:

1. Sāmaśramī, Satyavrata. The Śatapatha Brāhmaṇa of the White Yajurveda, with the Commentary of Sāyaṇa Ācārya. Nine volumes. Calcutta, 1899-1911 [Bibliotheca Indica].

Note: Only volumes 1-3, 5-7 were finished.

2. Śāstri, A. Chinnaswami. Śatapatha Brāhmaṇa: Mādhyandina Recension. Benares, 1937 [Kashi Sanskrit Series, no. 127].

3. Śatapatha Brāhmaṇa: Vājasaneyi Mādhyandina. Bombay: Laxmi-Venkateshwar Steam Press, 1940.

4. Weber, A. The Śatapatha-Brāhmaṇa in the Mādhyandina Śākhā with Extracts from the Commentaries of Sāyaṇa, Harisvāmin, and Dvivedaganga. Second edition. Varanasi: Chowkhamba Sanskrit Series Office, 1964 [Chowkhamba Sanskrit Series, no. 96: reprint of the 1855 edition].

The work has been translated by Julius Eggeling, entitled, The Śatapatha-Brāhmaṇa according to the Text of the Mādhyandina School. Five volumes. Delhi: Motilal Banarsidass, 1963 [reprint of the Sacred Books of the East

Series, volumes 12 (1882), 26 (1885), 41 (1894), 43 (1897), and 44 (1899)]. With reference to this translation see W. Caland, "Corrections of Eggeling's Translation of the Śatapatha Brāhmaṇa," _Bulletin of the School of Oriental and African Studies_, 6 (1931).

The _Kāṇvīya_ recension has been edited by W. Caland [_The Śatapatha Brāhmaṇa in the Kāṇvīya Recension_. Volume 1. Lahore: Motilal Banarsi-dass, 1926 (The Punjab Sanskrit Series, no. 10)] and Raghu Vira [_Śatapatha Brāhmaṇa in the Kāṇvīya Recension_. Volumes 2 and 3. Lahore, 1939]. No translation is available.

III. Brāhmaṇa of the Atharvaveda

The sole Brāhmaṇa belonging to the Atharvaveda is the Gopatha Brāhmaṇa, a work consisting of two sections, the first containing five prapāṭhaka's and the second containing six prapāṭhaka's. The work is a late derivative product taking passages from the Śatapatha, Aitareya, and Kauṣītaki Brāhmaṇa's.

The main editions are:

1. Gaastra, D. Das Gopatha Brāhmaṇa. Leiden, 1919.

2. Mitra, Rājendralāla and (continued by) H. Vidyābhūṣaṇa. The Gopatha Brāhmaṇa of the Atharva-Veda in the original Sanskrit. Calcutta, 1872 [Bibliotheca Indica]. Reprinted in 1972 by the Indological Book House (Delhi).

3. Trivedi, Kshemakaranadas. The Gopatha Brāhmaṇa. Allahabad, 1924.

The only English translation of this work is an unpublished Ph.D. thesis by Hukam Chand Patyal, entitled Gopatha Brāhmaṇa: English translation with notes and introduction. University of Poona, 1969.

Two important reference works by Maurice Bloomfield should be noted here. The first is his "Position of the Gopatha-Brāhmaṇa in Vedic Literature," JAOS 19:1f. The second is The Atharva-Veda and the Gopatha-Brāhmaṇa, Strassburg: Verlag von Karl J. Trübner, 1899 [Grundriss der Indo-Arischen Philologie und Altertumskunde. II. Band, 1. Heft, B].

# CHAPTER THREE

## ĀRAṆYAKA'S

The term Āraṇyaka means 'relating to, pertaining to, the forest (áraṇya-)', and is usually translated as 'forest-book, forest-treatise, forest-text.' Now the exact meaning of the word Āraṇyaka is based upon two slightly differing interpretations by Sāyaṇa. In his commentary to the Aitareya Brāhmaṇa [the preface portion: cited by Theodor Aufrecht, Das Aitareya Brāhmaṇa. Bonn: Adolf Marcus, 1879, p. iii] he writes: atha mahāvratam ity-ādikam ācāryā ācāryā ity antam āraṇyaka-vrata-rūpaṃ ca brāhmaṇam āvir abhūd iti 'Now the Mahāvrata (rite: beginning of Aitareya Āraṇyaka), etc. up to the (words): "ācāryā ācāryāḥ" [Ait. Ā 3.2.6] is presented to the Brāhman assuming the forest-vow [i.e., a Brāhman about to enter the third stage of life or āśrama: = vānaprastha].'

Sāyaṇa's second explanation appears in his preface to the Aitareya Āraṇyaka, he states:

aitareyabrāhmaṇe 'sti kāṇḍam
Āraṇyakā-'bhidham; araṇya eva
pāṭhyatvāt āraṇyakam iti-''ryate [5]*

'(There) is a section in the
Aitareya Brāhmaṇa called the
Āraṇyaka; it is proclaimed Āraṇyaka
because it is recited only in the forest.'

And:

sattra-prakaraṇe 'nuktir aranyā-'dhyayanāya
hi; mahāvratasya tasyā-'tra hautraṃ
karma vivicyate. [8]**

'Because (this) learning is intended to take place in the forest, expressing (this learning) is improper in the province of the home; the function pertaining to the Hotṛ's office is described here with regard to the Mahāvrata (rite).'

A similar statement also exists in Sāyaṇa's preface to his commentary on the Taittirīya Āraṇyaka, vs. 6 [araṇyā-'dhyayanād etad āraṇyakam itī-''ryate; araṇye tad adhīyīte- 'ty evaṃ vākyaṃ pravakṣyate].

Of the two explanations the first [the taking-up on the part of the Brāhman of the third stage of life] has little or no positive evidence to support it. The second, and more common, explanation of Sāyaṇa's seems more justified. A.B. Keith [The Aitareya Āraṇyaka, pp. 15-16] observes that:

> "The Āraṇyaka seems originally to have existed to give secret explanations of the ritual, and to have presupposed that the ritual was still in use and was known. No doubt the tendency was for the secret explanation to grow independent of the ritual until the stage is reached where the Āraṇyaka passes into the Upaniṣad, and contemporaneously the life of the Hindu is differentiated into the four Aśramas. But originally an Āraṇyaka must have merely meant a book of instruction to be given in the forest."

From the explanation above we may describe an Āraṇyaka as a sacrificial text which emphasizes the 'mystical' or secret and speculative aspects of certain sacrifices. It is to be looked upon as a more advanced study of the Vedic sacrifice which could only be mastered after the student became familiar with the Brāhmaṇa's.

Like the Brāhmaṇa's, the Āraṇyaka's belong to the various Vedic schools, whose names are evident of this fact. Thus the titles of the two Ṛgveda Āraṇyaka's are Aitareya and Kauṣītaki (or Śāṅkhāyana), both connected to the Brāhmaṇa's of the same name; the Sāmaveda Āraṇyaka is the Jaiminīya (or Talavakāra)-Upaniṣad-Brāhmaṇa belonging to the Jaiminīya Brāhmaṇa [see pages 26-27]; and the sole Kṛṣṇa Yajurveda Āraṇyaka is the Taittirīya Āraṇyaka, which is a continuation of the Taittirīya Brāhmaṇa-. The other schools do not possess independent Āraṇyaka's.

*This passage is found in Keith, Aitareya Āraṇyaka, p. 15. The Ānandāśrama edition has a variant reading for Padas c and d: araṇya eva paṭhyam syād āraṇyakam iti-"ryatām [the misprint itiryatām is corrected in the Śuddhāśuddha-patrikā].

**Keith, p. 15. The Ānandāśrama edition has a slightly different reading for Padas a and b: satra-prakaraṇe 'nuktir araṇyā-'dhyayanād itī.

## A. Aitareya Āraṇyaka

This work consists of five parts [Āraṇyaka's]. The first part discusses the Mahāvrata rite both from the ritualistic and speculative points of view. The second part consists of two divisions. The first division [2.1-3] deals with speculations of the Uktha or Hymn [the Niṣkevalya Śastra: the praise or recitation of the midday libation of the Mahāvrata], and its identity with Prāṇa 'Life-breath' and Puruṣa 'Man'; the second division (2.4-6) is the Aitareya Upaniṣad. The third part—called saṃhitāyā upaniṣat 'the Upaniṣad or Secret teaching of the Saṃhitā (-text)'—discusses the various forms of the text: the nirbhuja or Saṃhitā-text proper, the pratṛṇṇa or Pada-pāṭha ('word-text'), and Ubhayamantareṇa or the Krama-Pāṭha ('step-text') as well as speculations on the stops, the sibilants, and vowels, i.e., speech in general. The fourth part consists of Mahānāmnī verses and the fifth part consists of a description of the Niṣkevalya Śastra.

The editions and translation of the Aitareya Āraṇyaka are the following:

1. Keith, Arthur Berriedale, editor and translator. The Aitareya Āraṇyaka. Oxford at the Clarendon Press, 1909 [Anecdota Oxoniensia: Aryan Series. Part IX]. Reprinted in 1969.

2. Mitra, Rājendralāla, editor. Aitareya Āraṇyaka with the Commentary of Sāyaṇa Āchārya. Calcutta: Asiatic Society of Bengal, 1876 [Bibliotheca Indica].

3. Aitareyāraṇyakam. Śrīmat-Sāyaṇācārya-viracita-bhāṣya-sametam. Etat pustakam Taḷekaro-'pahva-Narahara-Śāstribhiḥ saṃśodhitam. Tac ca Rāvabahādura ity upapada-dhāribhiḥ-Gaṅgādhara Bāpūrāva Kāḷe, Je. Pi. ity etaiḥ. Puṇyākhya-pattane: Ānandāśrama-saṃskṛta-Granthāvaliḥ. Granthāṅkah 39 [third edition], 1959.

B. Kauṣītaki [Śāṅkhāyana] Āraṇyaka

This Āraṇyaka is attached to the Brāhmaṇa of the same name. The subject matter contained therein parallels that of the Aitareya Āraṇyaka [as well as other Vedic texts]. Thus Chapters (Adhyāya's) 1 and 2 of the Śāṅkhāyana discuss the Mahāvrata rite and so correspond to Aitareya Āraṇyaka 1 and 5; Adhyāya's 7 and 8 of the Śāṅkhāyana correspond to Āraṇyaka 3 of the Aitareya. Adhyāya 9 contains a passage on the strife or rivalry of the sense-powers which parallels Chāndogya Upaniṣad 5.1 and Bṛhad-Āraṇyaka-Upaniṣad 6.1, 7-13. Adhyāya 10 deals with the Internal Agnihotra, of which paragraphs 2-8 vaguely parallel Chāndogya Upaniṣad 5.19-24. Adhyāya 11 deals with death and the portents of death. Adhyāya 12 contains verses corresponding to those found in the Śaunaka and Paippalāda Atharvaveda, Taittirīya

Saṃhitā, Taittirīya Āraṇyaka, and Ṛgveda. Adhyāya 13 discusses the Brahman offering and contains passages found in Bṛhad-Āraṇyaka Upaniṣad 4.4-5. Adhyāya 14 underlines the importance of studying and knowing the meaning of the Veda. Then follows the Vaṃśa or line of teachers [Adhyāya 15).

Chapters 3-6 form the Kauṣītaki Upaniṣad or, as it is sometimes called, the Kauṣītaki-Brāhmaṇa-Upaniṣad.

The editions and translation of the Śāṅkhāyana are:

1. Keith, Arthur Berriedale, translator. The Śāṅkhāyana Āraṇyaka with an Appendix on the Mahāvrata. London: The Royal Asiatic Society, 1908 [Oriental Translation Fund. New Series, vol. 18].

2. Ṛgvedāntargataṃ Śāṅkhāyanāraṇyakam. Dekkana-kāleja-stha-gīrvāṇa-bhāṣādhyāpakaiḥ Pāṭhako-'pāhva-Śrīdhara-Śāstribhiḥ prastāvanā-pāṭha-bhedādibhiḥ saṃskṛtaṃ saṃśodhitam. Puṇyākhya-paṭṭane. Ānandāśrama-saṃskṛta-granthāvaliḥ. Granthāṅkaḥ 90, 1922.

C. Jaiminīya (or Talavakāra) Upaniṣad Brāhmaṇa

It has already been mentioned [p. 27] that this work (consisting of four chapters or Anuvāka's) is attached to the Jaiminīya Brāhmaṇa. Because this Āraṇyaka belongs to the Sāmaveda, there is emphasis upon speculative and secret teachings on that topic that would most interest a member of that school: the sāman-.

The Jaiminīya often introduces teleological myths to explain both the origin of the cosmos and speech (especially chanted speech). For instance, it begins with a myth relating how Prajapati won (ajayat) this (universe) with the three-fold Veda. Then he took the sap (rása-) of the three Vedas and upon uttering the Vyāhṛti's (bhūḥ, bhuvaḥ, suvaḥ) he extracted the sap from the Ṛg-, Yajur-, and Sāma-veda's, and this sap became respectively the earth, atmosphere, and sky. Presumably, the essence or sap of the latter three became fire (Agni), wind (Vāyu), and the sun (Āditya). But the myth does not stop here. There was one syllable (akṣára-) that the Primeval Father, despite all of his knowledge (Veda), could not extract from the sap: the syllable OM. Now this syllable is speech (vā́c-), and the essence (sap: rása-) of speech is the life-breath (prāṇá-). According to 1.2, 1 the syllable OM is the fire and speech the earth; OM is the wind and speech the atmosphere; OM is the sun and speech the sky; OM is the life-breath and speech is only (eva) speech. The purpose of this statement in setting up a correspondence between the cosmic elements and the syllable which introduces the Udgītha [the principal part of the sáman- chanted by the Udgātṛ́ priest; the other parts of the sāman- include basically the Prastāva or prelude sung by the Prastotṛ́ priest, the Pratihāra 'response (?)'; 'closing portion (?)' sung by the Pratihartṛ́, and the Nidhana or 'finale' sung by all three] is to emphasize the belief that the ultimate basis of the universe is OM [compare 1.8; 1.10; 1.18, 10-11].

Besides containing speculations on the syllable OM, this Āraṇyaya also contains important myths and legends such as the contention between the devá's and ásura's (1.15: Sharma's edition), a myth asserting that only the atmosphere existed in the beginning [1.20: Oertel's edition], the story of Bhageratha Aikṣvāka [4.6], the myth of the dispute among the six self-existing divinities regarding their preeminence [4.11f.: Oertel; 4.8f.: Sharma], the myth asserting that only space [áśā 'regions'] existed in the beginning [4.22: Oertel], and the story of Uccaiśśravas Kaupayeya [3.29f.: Oertel; 3.6: Sharma].

The editions and translation of this work are:

1. Limaye, V.P. and R.D. Vadekar, editors. Eighteen Principal Upaniṣads. Poona: Vaidika Saṃśodhana Maṇḍala, 1958.

Note: The work is simply called Jaiminīya Upaniṣad and appears between pages 377-474.

2. Oertel, Hanns, editor and translator. "The Jaiminīya or Talavakāra Upaniṣad Brāhmaṇa," JAOS 16 (1896):79-260.

3. Sharma, B.R. [II.II.F,6: p. 30].

D. Taittirīya Āraṇyaka

The Taittirīya Āraṇyaka is a true continuation of the Taittirīya Brāhmaṇa which, in turn, is itself a continuation of the Taittirīya Saṃhitā. As a result it resembles a Brāhmaṇa in subject-matter rather than a true Āraṇyaka. The contents are divided into ten chapters (Prapāṭhaka's). These contents are as follows:

Chapter 1: Mantra and brāhmaṇa for 'the Āruṇaketuka fire-piling.'

Chapter 2.1-2: brāhmaṇa and a few mantra's on svādhyāya 'recitation and repetition [= self-study] of the Veda.'

2.3-6: Mantra's for the Kuṣmāṇḍa Homa for the destruction of evil (Sāyaṇa to 2.3: pāpa-kṣayā-'rtham).

2.7-8: brāhmaṇa on the Kuṣmāṇḍa Homa.

2.9: brāhmaṇa on svādhyāya.

2.10-13: The Brahma-yajña (one of the five great sacrifices, according to TĀ 2.10).

2.14-15: Interruption of svādhyāya of the Brahma-yajña.

2.16-18: Prāyaścitta's or expiations.

2.19-20: brāhmaṇa and mantra: Upasthāna ('reverence'; 'devotion') [Sāyaṇa: of Brahman and the directions (diś-)].

Chapter 3.1: Mantra employed in the Cāturhotra piling (of the fire-altar).

3.2: Caturhotṛ Mantra.

3.3: Pañcahotṛ Mantra.

3.4: Ṣaḍḍhotṛ Mantra.

3.5: Saptahotṛ Mantra.

3.6: the second Ṣaḍḍhotṛ Mantra.

3.7: the Paryāya Mantra.

3.8: the Sambhāra sacrificial formulae (yajūṃṣi).

3.9: Devapatnī Mantra's.

3.10: Pratigraha Mantra's.

3.11: Daśahotṛ-hṛdaya Mantra.

Note: the Mantra's in 3.1-11 are employed in the Cāturhotra-piling [Sāyaṇa in his preface to 3.12].

3.12: *Brahmamedha* [according to Bharadvāja] or fire-piling *Mantra's* [according to Āpastambha].

3.13: *Puruṣamedha* stanzas.

3.14: Sāyaṇa entitles this *Anuvāka Bhartṛ-sūkta* 'the hymn to the Supporter.' These verses may be used for the animal sacrifice [Āpastamba].

3.15-21: The *Brahmamedha* [according to Bharadvāja]. Sāyaṇa entitles 3.15 the *Mṛtyu-sūkta* 'the hymn to Death.'

Chapter 4.1-42: *Pravargya Mantra's*.

Chapter 5.1-12: *brāhmaṇa* and verses belonging to the *Pravargya* rite

Chapter 6.1-12: *Pitṛmedha Mantra's*.

Chapters 7-9: *Taittirīya Upaniṣad*.

Chapter 10: *Nārāyaṇa Upaniṣad* [or *Mahā-Nārāyaṇa Upaniṣad*].

The editions of the *Taittirīya Āraṇyaka* include the following:

1. Mitra, Rājendralāla. *The Taittirīya Āraṇyaka of the Black Yajur Veda*. Calcutta, 1864-1872 [*Bibliotheca Indica*].

2. Śāstrī, Mahādeva and P.K. Rangāchārya. *The Taittirīya Āraṇyaka with the Commentary of Bhaṭṭabhāskaramiśra*. Three volumes. Mysore, 1900-1902.

3. *Kṛṣṇayajurvedīyaṃ Taittirīyāraṇyakam*. Śrīmat-Sāyaṇācārya-viracita-bhāṣya-sametam. Etat pustakaṃ "M.M. Prādhyāpaka Kāśīnātha Vāsudeva Abhyaṃkara-Śāstrī, M.A. Viśvas ta Ānandāśrama-saṃsthā" tathā "Paṃ. Ga. Aṃ. Jośī-Śāstrī . . . ity etaiḥ pāṭhabhedais saha saṃśodhitam. Puṇyākhya-pattane. Ānandāśrama-saṃskṛta-granthāvalih. Granth-āṅkah 36. Two volumes [third edition], 1967 and 1969.

## CHAPTER FOUR

## UPANIṢAD'S

The fourth and final portion of the Veda consists of a series of relatively short works called *Upaniṣad's*. This title is derived from the root *sad* 'to sit' and the prefixes *upa* 'near to,' 'by the side of,' and *ni* 'down': hence, 'to sit down near to (someone).' The sense of the word reflects the instruction of the student by the teacher of confidential, private, or secret doctrines. Thus it refers to the sitting of the student near to the teacher, the proximity reflecting a secret doctrine imparted by the latter to the former. From the basis of this description we may translate *Upaniṣad* as 'Secret Instruction'; 'Secret Meaning'; and even 'Secret Word' [see Paul Deussen, *The Philosophy of the Upanisads*, N.Y.: Dover Publications, 1966 (reprint of 1906 edition), pp. 10-17, especially pp. 16-17].

The number of *Upaniṣad's* numbers around 112 [Winternitz (*A History of Indian Literature*,[3] Vol. I, Part 1, Calcutta, 1962, p. 208) maintains that there are over 200 *Upaniṣad's*] but most of these compositions are sectarian religious works which are post-Vedic in both language and content. The purely Vedic *Upanisad's* as far as age, language, subject-matter, and/or position (those that are interwoven with the *Brāhmaṇa's* and *Āraṇyaka's*) are the following works:

1. *Bṛhad-Āraṇyaka-Upaniṣad*--contained in the concluding portion of the *Śatapatha Brāhmaṇa* (Chapter 14 of the *Mādhyaṃdina* recension: *ŚBM* 14.4-9. = *BĀU* 1-6).

2. *Chāndogya Upaniṣad* (see p. 30: *Mantra Brāhmaṇa*).

3. *Aitareya Upaniṣad* (see p. 43: *Aitareya Āraṇyaka*).

4. *Kauṣītaki Upaniṣad* (see p. 44: *Kauṣītaki Āraṇyaka*).

5. *Taittirīya Upaniṣad* (see p. 47: *Taittirīya Āraṇyaka*).

6. *Kena* (or *Talavakāra*) *Upaniṣad* (= *Jaiminīya Upaniṣad Brāhmaṇa* 4.18-21: Oertel's edition; not in Sharma's edition).

All these works are composed completely in prose, with the exception of the *Kena* which contains metrical portions.

The next group of *Upaniṣad's*, composed in verse and of later date, are attached to earlier Vedic works but are not an integral part of those works. The titles within this group are:

1. *Kaṭha (Kāṭhaka) Upaniṣad* (assigned to the Black Yajurvedic school of that name). This work may have been composed in the sixth century B.C. prior to the rise of the Buddha's teaching.

2. *Īśa (Īśāvāsya) Upaniṣad* (attached to the *Vājasaneyi Saṃhitā* of the White Yajur Veda (Chapter 40 of *VS*, the last Chapter or *Adhyāya* of this *Saṃhitā*). This *Upaniṣad*, sometimes called the *Vājasaneyi Saṃhitā Upaniṣad*, has no connection with the *Saṃhitā* as far as content is concerned.

3. *Mahānārāyaṇa Upaniṣad* (= *Taittirīya Āraṇyaka* 10: see p. 47). Whether or not this *Upaniṣad* was composed in the Vedic period is very uncertain. The work is included only because it is included within the *Taittirīya Āraṇyaka*.

All the other *Upaniṣads* may be considered--for lack of positive evidence--post-Vedic.

The Vedic *Upanisads* are, for the most part, dialogues or discussions on the true nature of reality, called either *brahman-* or *ātman-*, which underlies both the psycho-physical microcosm and the macrocosm.

Turning now to the individual editions and translations of the above-mentioned *Upaniṣads*, it must be emphasized that this is but a selected listing taken from a vast literature on this topic.

A. *Bṛhad-Āraṇyaka-Upaniṣad*

1. Editions

a. *Bṛhad-āraṇyako-'paniṣat*. Ānandagiri-kṛta-ṭīkā-saṃvalita-Śāṃkara-bhāṣya-sametā. Etat pustakaṃ Ve° Śā° Rā° Rā° "Kāśīnātha Śāstrī Āgāśe" ity etaiḥ saṃśodhitam. Puṇyākhya-pattane: Ānandāśrama-saṃskṛta-granthāvaliḥ. Granthāṅkaḥ 15 (fourth edition), 1939.

b. Böhtlingk, Otto von, editor and translator. *Bṛhadāraṇyakopaniṣad in der Mādhyaṃdina-Recension*. Petersburg, 1889-1890.

c. Gambhirananda, Swami, editor and translator. Bṛhadāraṇyaka Upaniṣad. Calcutta: Udbodhan Office, 1944.

d. Joshi, Vasudeva Mahashankar. Bṛhadāraṇyaka-Upaniṣad. Two volumes. Ahmedabad: Sastu Sahitya, 1963-1964.

e. Radhakrishnan, S., editor and translator, The Principal Upaniṣads. N.Y.: Humanities Press, Inc., 1953 (1968).

f. Sénart, Émile, editor and translator. Bṛhad-Āraṇyaka-Upaniṣad. Paris: Societé d'Édition "Les Belles Lettres," 1967 [reprinted from the 1934 edition].

g. Vasu, Srisa Chandra, editor and translator. The Brihad-aranyaka-Upanisad; with the Commentary of Sri Madhvacharya, called also Anandatirtha. Allahabad: Pāṇini Office, 1916 [Sacred Books of the Hindus, Volume 14].

Note: The Sacred Books of the Hindus have been reprinted in 1974 by the AMS Press, Inc., 56 East 13th Street, New York, N.Y. 10003.

2. Translations

a. Böhtlingk [1.b].

b. Deussen, Paul, Sechzig Upanishads des Veda. Third edition. Leipzig: F. A. Brockhaus, 1921.

c. Gambhirananda [1.c].

d. Hume, Robert Ernest. The Thirteen Principal Upanishads. Second edition. Oxford University Press, 1965.

e. Mādhavānanda, Swāmī, translator. Bṛhadāraṇyaka Upaniṣad; with the Commentary of Śaṅkarācārya. Fourth edition. Calcutta, 1965.

f. Müller, F. Max. The Upaniṣads. Volume two. N.Y.: Dover Publications, Inc., 1962 [reprinted from the Sacred Books of the East Series, vol. 15 (1884)].

g. Radhakrishnan [1.e].

h. Röer, E. The Brihad Aranyaka Upanishad with the commentary of Sankara Āchārya and the gloss of Ānanda Giri. Three volumes. Calcutta: Asiatic Society of Bengal, 1849 [vols. 1 and 2], 1856 [vol. 3] [Bibliotheca Indica]. This work contains both the text and translation of the Kāṇvīya recension.

i. Vasu [1.g].

j. Vidyasagara, Jibananda. Bṛhad-Āraṇyaka Upaniṣad, with the Commentary of Sankaracharya and the Gloss of Ānandagiri. Calcutta, 1875.

3. Other titles of interest

a. Bhatt, V.P. "Concept of Prāṇa in the Bṛhadāraṇyaka Upaniṣad," Pandit Rajeshwar Sastri Dravid Felicitation Volume. Edited by Devadatta Sastri, et. al. Allahabad: Bharati Parisad, 1971, pp. 134-144.

b. Brahma, Nalini Kanta. "Studies in the Brihadaranyaka Upanishad," Prabuddha Bhārata (Almora) 56:19-381.

c. Bṛhad-āraṇyako-'paniṣad-bhāṣya-vārtikam. Ānandagiri-kṛta-śāstra-prakāśikākhya-ṭīkā-saṃvalitam. Etat pustakaṃ Ve° Śā° Rā° Rā° "Kāśīnātha-Śāstri Āgāśe" ity etaiḥ saṃśodhitam. Puṇyākhya-pattane: Ānandāśrama-saṃskṛta-granthāvaliḥ. Granthāṅkaḥ 16 (second edition), 1937.

d. Deussen, Paul. The Philosophy of the Upanishads. Translated into English by A.S. Geden. N.Y.: Dover Publications, Inc., 1966 [reprinted from the 1906 edition].

e. Keith, Arthur Berriedale, The Religion and Philosophy of the Veda and Upanishads. Volume Two. Cambridge, Mass.: Harvard University Press, 1925 [Harvard Oriental Series, vol. 32]. Reprinted in 1971 by Motilal Banarsidass (Delhi).

f. Mahadevan, T.M.P., The Upanishads, Selections from the 108 Upanishads with English Translation. Madras: G.A. Natesan and Co., n.d.

g. Oldenberg, Hermann, Die Lehre der Upanishaden und die Anfänge des Buddhismus. Göttingen: Vandenhoeck and Ruprecht, 1915.

h. Raju, P.T. "The Psychology of the Bṛhadāraṇyaka Upaniṣad," Journal of Oriental Research (Madras) 15 (4), pp. 173-182.

i. Rau, Wilhelm. "Zur Text-Kritik der Bṛhadāraṇyakopaniṣad," Zeitschrift der Deutschen Morgenländischen Gesellschaft (Wiesbaden), 105 (2), pp. 58f.

j. Ruben, W. Die Philosophen der Upanishaden. Bern: A. Francke AG, 1947.

B. Chāndogya-Upaniṣad

1. Editions

a. Böhtlingk, Otto von, editor and translator. Chāndogyopaniṣad. Leipzig, 1889.

b. Chāndogyo-'paniṣat. Ānandagiri-kṛta-ṭīkā-saṃvalita-Śāṃkara-bhāṣya-sametā. Ratnāgiri-grāma-nivāsi 'Mahāmaho-' pādhyāya' ity upapada-dhāri-Bālaśāstrisūri-sūnubhiḥ 'Agāśe' ity upāhvaiḥ Ve° Sā° Saṃ° Rā° Rā° Kāśinātha-Śāstribhiḥ saṃśodhita. Puṇyākhya-pattane: Ānandāśrama-saṃskṛta-granthāvaliḥ. Granthāṅkaḥ 14 (fifth edition), 1934.

c. Chāndogyo-'paniṣad. Nityānanda-kṛta-mitākṣarā-vyākhyā-sametā. Ve° Śā° Rā° Vaidyo-'pāhvai Raṃganātha-Śāstribhiḥ saṃśodhitā. Puṇyākhya-pattane: Ānandāśrama-saṃskṛta-granthāvaliḥ. Granthāṅkaḥ 79, 1915.

d. Gambhirananda, Swami, editor and translator (into Bengāli). Chāndogyopanisad. Calcutta: Udbodhan Office, 1943.

e. Jha, Ganganatha, editor and translator. Chāndogyopaniṣad. Poona: Oriental Book Agency, 1942.

Note: Śaṃkara's commentary is translated in this text.

f. Radhakrishan [A.1.e].

g. Röer, E. The Chāndogya Upanishad with the commentary of Sankara Āchārya, and the gloss of Ānanda Giri. Calcutta, 1849-1850 [Bibliotheca Indica].

h. Senart, Emile. Chāndogya Upaniṣad. Paris, 1930 [text with French translation].

i. Swāhānanda, Swami, editor and translator. Chāndogya Upaniṣad. Madras: Ramakrishna Ashram, 1956.

j. Vasu, Śriśa Chandra, editor and translator. Chhạndogya Upanisad; with the commentary of Śrī Madhvāchārya, called also Ananda-tirtha. Allahabad: Pāṇini Office, 1910 [Sacred Books of the Hindus, Volume 3]. Reprinted by the AMS Press (N.Y.), 1974. See note to A.1.g.

2. Translations

a. Böhtlingk [B.1.a].

b. Deussen [A.2.b].

c. Hume [A.2.d].

d. Mitra, Rajendralala. Chandogya Upanishad of the Sama Veda, with extracts from the Commentary of Sankara Āchārya. Calcutta, 1862 [Bibliotheca Indica].

e. Müller, F. Max. The Upaniṣads. Volume One. N.Y.: Dover Publications, Inc., 1962 [reprinted from the Sacred Books of the East Series, vol. 1 (1879)].

f. Radhakrishnan [A.1.e].

g. Senart [B.1.h].

h. Swāhānanda Swami [B.1.i].

i. Vasu [B.1.j].

3. Other titles of interest

a. Carpani, E.G. "A Sanskrit Index to the Chāndogya Upaniṣad," New Indian Antiquary (Bombay), I-III (1938-1941), [in installments].

b. Carpani, E.G. "A Philosophical Index to the Chāndogya Upaniṣad," Indian Culture (Calcutta), 4 and 6 (July, 1937 and July, 1939), [in installments].

c. Hauschild, Richard. "Über altbekannte und neuentdeckte metrische Stücke in the Chāndogya-Upaniṣad," Die Sprache 7 (1961): 32-61.

d. Tyagisananda, Swami. "The Chāndogya Upaniṣad," Vedanta Kesara (Madras), vols. 33-34, pp. 52-57, 104-109, 179-183, 250-256; [vol. 34], pp. 26-33, 71-77, 133-137, 191-198, 268-273, 299-304, 339-344.

C. Aitareya Upaniṣad

1. Editions

a. Aitareyo-'paniṣat. Ānandagiri-kṛta-ṭīkā-saṃvalita-Śāṃkara-bhāṣya-sametā; tathā Vidyāraṇya-viracitai-"tareyo-'paniṣad-dīpikā ca. Etat pustakam Ānandāśrama-stha-paṇḍitaiḥ saṃśodhitam. Puṇyākhya-pattane: Ānandāśrama-saṃskṛta-granthāvaliḥ. Granthāṅkaḥ 11 [fifth edition], 1931.

b. Gambhirānanda, Swami, editor and translator. Eight Upaniṣads. Volume two. Second edition. Calcutta: Advaita Ashrama, 1966 [With the translated commentary of Śaṅkarācārya].

c. Keith [Chapter Three, A.1: p. 43].

d. Mitra [Chapter Three, A.2: p. 43].

e. Radhakrishnan [Chapter Four, A.1.e].

f. Sharvananda, Swami, editor and translator. Aitareya Upaniṣad. Madras: Ramakrishna Math, 1967.

g. Silburn, Lilian, editor and translator. Aitareya Upaniṣad. Paris: Adrien-Maisonneuve, 1950 [Les Upanishad, Part X: translation and notes in French].

h. Venkataramiah, D., editor and translator. Aitareyopaniṣad with the bhāṣya of Śaṃkara. Bangalore, 1934.

i. Vidyarnava, Rai Bahadur Srisa Chandra and Pandit Mohan Lal Sandal, editors and translators. Aitareya Upanisat. Allahabad: Major B.D. Basu at the Pāṇini Office, 1925 [Sacred Books of the Hindus, vol. 30, part 1]. Reprinted by AMS Press (N.Y.), 1974.

2. Translations

a. Bhakkamkar, H.M. Aitareyopaniṣad with Śaṅkara's bhāṣya. Bombay: Univ. of Bombay, 1899 [reprinted and published by R.G. Bhakkamkar. Dharwar, 1922].

b. Deussen [Chapter Four, A.2.b].

c. Gambhirānanda [C.1.b].

d. Hume [A.2.d].

e. Keith [Chapter Three, A.1].

f. Mitra [Chapter Three, A.2].

g. Müller [Chapter Four, B.2.e].

h. Radhakrishnan [A.1.e].

i. Röer, E. The Upanishads. Taittiriya, Aitareya, Svetasvatara, Isa, Kena, Katha, Prasna, Mundaka, and Mandukya. Calcutta, 1851-1855 [Bibliotheca Indica; new edition edited by Manmatha Nath Dutt, 1907].

j. Sharvananda [C.1.f].

k. Silburn [C.1.g].

l. Venkataramiah [C.1.h].

m. Vidyarnava [C.1.i].

3. Other title of interest

a. Schneider, Ulrich. "Die Komposition der Aitareya-Upaniṣad," Indo-Iranian Journal 7 (1963):58-69.

D. Kauṣītaki Upaniṣad

1. Editions

a. Cowell, E.B., editor and translator. Kaushitaki-Brahmana-Upanishad, with the Commentary of Sankarananda. Calcutta, 1861 [Bibliotheca Indica]. Reprinted in 1968 by Chowkhamba Sanskrit Series Office (Varanasi) [Chowkhamba Sanskrit Studies, vol. 64].

b. Frenz, A. "Kauṣītaki Upaniṣad," Indo-Iranian Journal 11 (1969):72-129.

c. Radhakrishnan [Chapter Four, A.1.e].

d. Renou, Louis, editor and translator. Kauṣītaki Upaniṣad. Paris: Adrien-Maisonneuve, 1948 [Les Upanishad, Part VI].

c. Vidyarnava, Srisa Chandra and Pandit Mohan Lal Sandal, editors and translators. The Kausitaki Upanisat. Allahabad: Major B.D. Basu at the Pāṇini Office, 1925 [Sacred Books of the Hindus, vol. 31, part 1]. Reprinted by AMS Press (N.Y.), 1974.

2. Translations

a. Cowell [D.1.a].

b. Deussen [Chapter Four, A.2.b].

c. Hume [A.2.d].

d. Keith [Chapter Three, B.1].

e. Müller [Chapter Four, B.2.e].

f. Radhakrishnan [A.1.e].

g. Renou [D.1.d].

h. Vidyarnava [D.1.e].

3. Other titles of interest

a. Antoine, R. "Religious Symbolism in the Kauṣītaki Upaniṣad," JOI (Baroda), vol. 4 (4), pp. 330-337.

b. Bhattacharya, Sivaprasad. "A passage in the Kauṣītaki-brāhmaṇopaniṣad (I.2-6): some suggestions as to the proper readings and a clue to its import." Proceedings of the All India Oriental Conference (16th session), Lucknow 1951, pp. 1-9 [also in the Poona Orientalist, vol. 15, pp. 130-142].

c. Thieme, Paul. "Der Weg durch den Himmel nach der Kauṣītaki-Upaniṣad" Wissenschaftliche Zeitschrift der Martin Luther Univ. (Halle-Wittenberg), Vol. 1 (3), Gesellschafts und Sprachwissenschaftliche Reihe No. 1 (1951-1952), pp. 19-36.

E. Taittirīya Upaniṣad

1. Editions

a. Gambhirananda, Swami, editor and translator. Eight Upaniṣads. Volume one. Calcutta: Advaita Ashrama, 1957.

b. Gokhale, Diṇker Vishnu. Shrī Sankarāchārya's Taittiriyopanishad-bhāshya With the gloss of Ānandagiri. Bombay, 1914.

c. Lesimple, Em., editor and translator. Taittirīya Upaniṣad. Paris: Adrien-Maissoneuve, 1948 [Les Upanishad, Part IX].

d. Radhakrishnan [A.1.e].

e. Sastri, A. Mahadeva. The Taittirīya Upanishad, with the Commentaries of Śankarāchārya, Sureśvarāchārya, and Sāyaṇa (Vidyāraṇya). Mysore: G.T.A. Printing Works, 1903 [translated into English].

f. Sharvananda, Swami. Taittirīyopaniṣad. Madras: Shri Ramakrishna Math, 1971 [text and English translation].

g. Tirtha, Sri Achyuta Krishnananda. Vanamala, a Commentary on the Taittiriyopanishad bhashya. Srirangam, 1913 [Śrīvāṇīvilāsa S. Ser. XIII].

h. Taittirīyo-'paṇiṣat. Ānandagiri-kṛta-ṭīkā-saṃvaliṭa-Sāṃkara-bhāṣyo-'petā. Paṇḍita Vāmana-Śāstrī Isalāṃapurakara ity etaiḥ saṃśodhitā. Tathā Śaṃkarānanda-kṛtā

Taittirīyo-'paniṣad-dīpikā. Etat pustakam Ānandāśrama-stha-paṇḍitaiḥ saṃśodhitam. Puṇyākhya-pattane: Ānandāśrama-saṃskṛta-granthāvaliḥ. Granthāṅkah 12 [fifth edition], 1929.

i. Vidyarnava, Srisa Chandra and Pandit Mohan Lal Sandal, editors and translators. The Taitiriya Upaniṣat. Allahabad: Major B.D. Basu at the Pāṇini Office, 1925 [Sacred Books of the Hindus, Vol. 30, Part 3]. Reprinted by the AMS Press (N.Y.), 1974.

2. Translations

a. Deussen [A.2.b].

b. Gambhirananda [E.1.a].

c. Hume [A.2.d].

d. Müller [A.2.f].

e. Lesimple [E.1.c].

f. Radhakrishnan [A.1.e].

g. Röer [C.2.i].

h. Sastri [E.1.e].

i. Sharvananda [E.1.f].

j. Vidyarnava [E.1.i].

3. Other works of interest

a. Boetzelaer, J.M. van, translator. Sureśvara's Taittirīyopaniṣad Bhāṣyavārtikam. Leiden: E.J. Brill, 1971 [Orientalia Rheno-Traiectina, vol. 12].

b. Gupta, Babu Ram. Taittirīya Varttika of Sureśvara: A Study. Allahabad: Allahabad University Studies, 1932.

c. Lommel, H. "Vedische Einzelheiten [über Taittirīya Upaniṣad III. Schluss. (Bhṛguvallī 7-10]" Zeitschrift der Deutschen Morgenländischen Gesellschaft (Wiesbaden), Vol. 99, pp. 43-49.

F. Kena [Talavakāra] Upaniṣad

1. Editions

a. Gambhirananda [E.1.a].

b. Keno-'paniṣat. Sa-ṭīkā-Śāṃkara-pada-vākya-bhāṣyo-'petā. Ratnāgiri-grāma-nivāsibhir veda-śāstrajñair Maho-'pādhyāyaiḥ Āgāśe ity upāhvair Bāla-Śāstribhiḥ saṃśodhitā. Tathā Śaṃkarānanda-kṛtā Keno-'paniṣad-dīpikā Nārāyaṇa-viracitā Keno-'paniṣad-dīpikā ca. Idaṃ pustaka-dvitayam Ānandāśrama-stha-paṇḍitaiḥ saṃśodhitam. Puṇyākhya-pattane: Ānandāśrama-saṃskṛta-granthāvaliḥ. Granthāṅkaḥ 6 [sixth edition], 1934.

c. Mahadevan, T.M.P., editor and translator. Kena Upaniṣad. Madras, 1958.

d. Oertel [Chapter Three, C.2: p. 45].

e. Radhakrishnan [A.1.e].

f. Renou, Louis, editor and translator, Kena Upanishad. Paris: Adrien-Maisonneuve, 1943 [Les Upanishad, Part III].

g. Röer, E. The Īśa, Kena, Kaṭha, Praśna, Muṇḍa, Māṇḍukya Upaniṣads, with the Commentary of Śankara Ācārya and the gloss of Ānandagiri. Calcutta, 1850 [Bibliotheca Indica].

h. Sharvananda, Swami, editor and translator. Kenopaniṣad. Madras: Ramakrishna Math, 1943.

i. Varadachari, K.C. Kenopaniṣad, With Raṅga-Rāmānuja-Bhāṣya. Tirupati, 1943.

j. Vasu, Srisa Chandra, editor and translator. The Upaniṣads; with the commentary of Madhvacharya. Part I: Containing Isa, Kena, Katha, Prasna, Mundaka, and Mandukya. Allahabad: Panini Office, 1909 [Sacred Books of the Hindus, Vol. 1]. The second edition came out in 1911 [Allahabad: Sudhīndranātha Vasu from the Pāṇini Office, 1911] and was reprinted by the AMS Press (N.Y.) in 1974.

2. Translations

a. Deussen [A.2.b].

b. Gambhirananda [E.1.a].

c. Hiriyanna, Mysore. Kenopanishad with the Commentary of Srī Sankarāchārya. Srirangam: Sri Vain Vials Press, 1912.

d. Hume [A.2.d].

e. Müller [B.2.e].

f. Oertel [Chapter Three, C.2].

g. Radhakrishnan [A.1.e].

h. Renou [F.1.f].

i. Röer [C.2.i].

j. Sharvananda [F.1.h].

k. Vasu [F.1.j].

3. Other titles of interest

a. Aurobindo, Sri. "Kena Upanishad," Sri Aurobindo Mandir Annual, Jayantī. No. 14 (1955), pp. 1-4.

b. Chaudhury, P.J. "Kena Upanishad," Prabuddha Bhārata (Almora) 59, pp. 547-550, 582-586.

c. Singh, Chhajju. Kainopanishat. Lahore: Anglo-Sanskrit Press, 1891.

d. Vidyārṇava, Rai Bahadur Śrīśa Chandra. Studies in the First Six Upanisads; The Isa and Kena Upanisads with the Commentary of Sankara. Allahabad: Sudhīndra Nātha Vasu at the Pāṇini Office, 1919 [Sacred Books of the Hindus, Vol. 22, Part 1]. This edition has been reprinted by the AMS Press (N.Y.), in 1974.

G. Kaṭha (Kāṭhaka) Upaniṣad

1. Editions

a. Bucca, S. "Katha-Upanishad," Revue de la Facutad de Filosofia y Letras (Univ. Nacional de Tucuman, Argentina), Vol. I (2) (1953), pp. 229-301.

b. Gambhirananda [E.1.a].

c. Kāṭhako-'paniṣat. Sa-ṭīkā-dvaya (Ānandagiri-Gopālayatīndra) Śāṃkara-bhāṣyo-'petā. Se-'yaṃ Māsṭara āph Ārṭs ity upapada-dhāribhiḥ Phargyusana-kaleja-stha-saṃskṛta-bhāṣā-'dhyāpakaiḥ "Rājavāḍe" ity upāhvair Vaijanātha-Śarmabhiḥ saṃśodhitā. Puṇyākhya-pattane: Ānandāśrama-saṃskṛta-granthāvaliḥ. Granthāṅkaḥ 7 [seventh edition], 1935.

d. Pelly, R.L. Kaṭha Upaniṣad: Introduction, Text, Translation, and Notes. Calcutta, 1924.

e. Radhakrishnan [A.1.e].

f. Renou, Louis, editor and translator. Katha Upanishad. Paris: Adrien-Maisonneuve, 1943 [Les Upanishad, Part 2].

g. Röer [F.1.g].

h. Sharvananda, Swami, editor and translator. Kaṭhopaniṣad. Seventh edition. Madras: Ramakrishna Math, 1952.

i. Vasu [F.1.j].

2. Translations

a. Bucca [G.1.a].

b. Deussen [A.2.b].

c. Edgerton, Franklin. The Beginnings of Indian Philosophy. Cambridge, Mass.: Harvard University Press, 1965.

d. Gambhirananda [E.1.a].

e. Hiriyanna, M. Kāṭhakopanishad with the Commentary of Srī Sankarācārya. Srirangam: Sri Vain Vials Press, 1915.

f. Hume [A.2.d].

g. Müller [A.2.f].

h. Otto, R. Die Kaṭha-Upaniṣad. Berlin: Töpelmann 1938 [Welt der Religions 24].

i. Pelly [G.1.d].

j. Radhakrishnan [A.1.e].

k. Renou [G.1.f].

l. Röer [C.2.i].

m. Sharvananda [G.1.h].

n. Vasu [F.1.j].

o. Whitney, W.D. "Translation of the Kaṭha-Upaniṣad," Transactions of the American Philological Association, 1890, pp. 88f.

3. Other titles of interest

a. Abhedananda, Swami. Mystery of Death: A Study in the Philosophy and Religion of the Kaṭha Upaniṣad. Calcutta: Ramakrishna Vedanta Math, 1967.

b. Alsdorf, L. "Contributions to the textual criticism of the Kathopanisad," Zeitschrift der Morgenländischen Gesellschaft 100 (1950):621-637.

c. Belloni-Filippi, F. La "Kāṭhaka-Upaniṣad," Pisa, 1905 [translation in Italian with a note on Indian pantheism].

d. Coomaraswamy, Anand K. "Notes on the Kaṭha Upaniṣad," New Indian Antiquary (Bombay), I (1938-1939), [April issue, pp. 43-56; May issue, pp. 83-108; June issue, pp. 199-213].

e. ______. "A study of the Kaṭha Upaniṣad," Indian Historical Quarterly (Calcutta) 11 (1935):570-584.

f. Glasenapp, Helmuth von. "Buddhism in the Kāṭhaka-Upaniṣad?" New Indian Antiquary 1 (1938-39):138-141 [May issue]. Also in his Von Buddha zu Gandhi (Wiesbaden: Harrassowitz, 1962), pp. 81-85.

g. Heimann, Betty. Madhva (Ānandatīrtha's) Kommentar zur Kāṭhaka-Upaniṣad. Sanskrit-Text in Transcription, nebst Übersetzung und Noten, Leipzig, 1922.

h. _______. "The Problem of the Kāṭhaka Upaniṣad," New Review (Calcutta), Vol. 9 (June, 1939).

i. Helfer, J.S. "The Initiatory Structure of the Kaṭhopaniṣad," History of Religions (Chicago) 7 (4) (May 1968):348-367.

j. Johnston, E.H. "On Some Difficulties of the Kaṭha Upaniṣad," A Volume of Eastern and Indian Studies presented to Professor F.W. Thomas, C.I.E., on his 72nd birth-day 21st March 1939. Bombay, 1939.

k. Mitra, S.K. "The Kaṭhopaniṣad: The story of Naciketas or Man's Search for his Soul," A.B. Dhruva Commemoration Volume. Ahmedabad, n.d.

l. Prem, Sri Krishna. The Yoga of the Kaṭhopaniṣad. Allahabad: Ananda Publishing House, 1943.

m. Rawson, J.N. The Kaṭha Upaniṣad. London: Oxford University Press, 1934.

n. Sarma, D.S. The Kaṭhopaniṣad and the Gītā. Madras: M.R. Sheshan, 1932.

o. Varadachari, K.C. and D.T. Tatacharya, editors and translators. Kaṭhopaniṣad Bhāṣyam of Śrī Raṅgarāmānuja. Tirupati, 1949 [Śrī Veṅkaṭeśvara Oriental Institute Series, no. 15].

p. Weller, Friedrich. "Versuch einer kritik der Kaṭhopaniṣad," Institut fur Orientforschung (Deutsche Akademie der Wissenschaft zu Berlin), No. 12, Akademie-Verlag, 1953, 229f.

q. Whitney, W.D. "Hindu Eschatology and the Kaṭha Upaniṣad," Proceedings of the American Oriental Society, 1886, pp. ciiif.

H. Īśa [Īśāvāsya] Upaniṣad

1. Editions

a. Baynes, H., editor and translator. "The Vājasaneya Upaniṣad," Indian Antiquary 26:213f.

b. Bucca, S. "Īśa Upaniṣad," Notas y Estudios de Filosofia (Argentina), 3 (9), 1952, pp. 47-55 [translation in Spanish].

c. Carpani, E.G. "Īśa Upaniṣad," Indian Culture 3 (July 1936).

d. Gambhirananda [E.1.a].

e. Gosvami, Sri Syamamala, editor and translator. Īśa-Upanishad: with the Bhāsyas of Baladeva Vidyabhusana. Calcutta, 1895.

f. Īśāvāsyo-'paniṣat. Ānandagiri-kṛta-ṭīkā-saṃvalita-Śāṃkara-bhāṣyo-'petā. Mahāmaho-'pādhyāyaiḥ Āgāśe ity upāhvair Bālaśāstribhiḥ saṃśodhitā. Brahmānanda-Ṣarasvatī-kṛtam Īśāvāsya-Rahasyam; Saṃkarānanda-kṛte-''śāvāsya-Dīpikā; Rāmacandra-Paṇḍita-kṛte-''śāvāsya-Rahasya-Vivṛtih. Etat pustaka-tritayam Ānandāśrama-stha-paṇḍitaiḥ saṃśodhitaṃ ca. Puṇyākhya-pattane: Ānandāśrama-saṃskṛta-granthāvaliḥ. Granthāṅkaḥ 5 [sixth edition], 1934.

g. Mahadevan, T.M.P., editor and translator. Īśāvasya Upaniṣad. Madras: Upanishad Vihar, Jayanti Series 2, 1957.

h. Majumdar, Jnanendralal, editor and translator. Īsha Upanishat with a new Commentary by the Kaulācharyya Sadānanda. London, 1918.

i. Majumdar, J. Īśopaniṣad (with the bhāṣya of Satyānanda). Madras: Ganesh and Co., 1953.

j. Radhakrishnan [A.1.e].

k. Renou, Louis. Isa Upanishad. Paris: Adrien-Maisonneuve, 1943 [Les Upanishad, Part 1: text and French translation].

l. Sarma, Y. Subrahmanya. Īśāvāsyopaniṣad. Bangalore: Adhyātma Prakāsa Office, 1932.

m. Sharvananda, Swami. Īśa Upaniṣad. Madras: Shri Ramakrishna Math, 1964.

n. Varadachari, K.C. and D.T. Tatacharya, editors and translators. Īśāvāsyopaniṣad with Veṅkaṭanātha's Bhāṣya. Tirupati, 1942 [Śrī Veṅkaṭeśvara Oriental Institute Series, no. 5].

o. Vasu [F.1.j].

p. Vira, Raghu. Īśa Upaniṣad. Lahore, 1937 [Sarasvati Vihara Series].

2. Translations

a. Baynes [h.1.a].

b. Bucca [H.1.2].

c. Carpani [H.1.3].

d. Deussen [A.2.b].

e. Gambhirananda [E.1.a].

f. Gosvami [H.1.e].

g. Griffith, Ralph T.H. The Texts of the White Yajurveda. Third edition. Banaras: Shri B.N. Yadav, Proprietor, E.J. Lazarus and Co., 1957 [reprint].

h. Hiriyanna, M. Īśāvāsyopaniṣad, with the Commentary of Śrī Śaṅkarācārya. Srirangam, 1911.

i. Hume [A.2.d].

j. Mahadevan [H.1.g].

k. Majumdar [H.1.h-i].

l. Müller [B.2.e].

m. Radhakrishnan [A.1.e].

n. Ramaswamier, S. The Vaja-Saneya-Samhitopanishad with the Bhashya of Srimat Sankaracharya. Madras: National Press, 1884.

o. Renou [H.1.k].

p. Sarma [H.1.1].

q. Sharvananda [H.1.m].

r. Varadachari [H.1.n].

s. Vasu [H.1.o].

3. Other titles of interest

a. Dhruva, B.M. "The Conception of Brahman in the Īśāvāsya Upaniṣad," Summary of Papers, 19th All India Oriental Conference (Poona), (Delhi, 1957), pp. 130-131.

b. Poucha, Pavel. "Īśāvāsyopaniṣad (Yajurveda 40). Über die Entwicklung eines upanischadischen Texts" Listy Filologické (Prague) 68 (1941):351-364 [also in Zeitschrift der Deutschen Morgenländischen Gesellschaft, 94, pp. 409-417.

c. Schrader, Otto. "A Critical Study of Īśopaniṣad," Indian Antiquary (Bombay) 62 (August-November 1933).

d. Strauss, O. "Scholastisches zum Anfang der Īśa Upaniṣad" Winternitz Commemoration Volume. Leipzig, 1933.

e. Thieme, Paul. "Īśopaniṣad (= Vājasaneyi-Saṁhitā 40, 1-14)," JAOS 85 (1965):89-99.

f. Varadachari, K.C. "Clue into the Understanding of Mystic and Religious Consciousness according to Īśāvāsyopaniṣad-Bhāṣya of Veṅkaṭanātha," 10th All-India Oriental Conference, Tirupati, 1940.

g. ______. "Īśāvāsyopaniṣad-Bhāṣya: A Study," Kane Commemoration Volume, Poona, 1941.

h. ______. "Meditation on the Īśāvāsyopaniṣad," Journal of the Ganganath Jha Research Institute (Allahabad), Vol. 3 (3-4), pp. 241-261.

I. Mahānārāyaṇa Upaniṣad

1. Editions and translations

a. Deussen [A.2.b].

b. See Chapter Three, D.1-3 (p. 47).

c. Varenne, J. La Mahā Nārāyaṇa Upaniṣad. Two volumes. Paris: Editions E de Boccard, 1960 [Publications de L'Institut de Civilisation Indienne, Fascicules 11 and 13].

d. Vimalananda, Swami. Mahānārāyaṇa Upaniṣad. Madras: Ramakrishna Math, 1957 [text, explanation in Sanskrit, word by word meaning, running translation, and notes]. Reprinted in 1968.

J. Collected editions

1. Daśo-paniṣadaḥ. (mūla-mātram). Etat pustakam Ve° Śā° Śaṃkara-Śāstrī Mārulakara ity etaiḥ saṃśodhitam. Puṇyākhya-pattane: Ānandāśrama-Saṃskṛta-granthāvaliḥ. Granthāṅkaḥ 106, 1937 [contains the Īśa, Kena, Kāṭhaka, Praśna, Muṇḍaka, Māndukya, Taittirīya, Aitareya, Chāndogya, and Bṛhadāraṇyaka Upaniṣads].

2. Harirātmaja, Keśavāla. Eleven Upanishads. Bombay: Nirṇaya-Sagara Press, 1886.

3. Īśa-Kena-Kaṭho-'paniṣadaḥ. Digambarānucara-viracitā-'rtha-prakāśākhya-vyākhyā-sametāḥ. Etat pustakaṃ Ḍekkana-kaleja-stha-saṃskṛtādhyāpakaiḥ Ve° Śā° Rā° Pāṭhako-'pāhvaiḥ śrīdhara-śāstribhiḥ Ānandāśrama-stha-paṇḍitaiś ca saṃśodhitam. Puṇyākhya-pattane: Ānandāśrama-saṃskṛta-granthāvaliḥ. Granthāṅkaḥ 76, 1945.

4. Limaye [Chapter Three, C.1: p. 45].

5. Paṇśīkar, Wasudev Laxmaṇ Shāstrī. One Hundred and Eight Upanishads (Īsha and Others). Fourth edition. Bombay: Pāndurang Jāwajī (Nirṇaya Sāgar Press), 1932.

6. Pitambara, Sri. Eight Upanishads. Bombay, 1890.

7. Sastri, S. Sitarama and Ganganath Jha. The Upanishads and Sri Sankara's Commentary. Five volumes. Madras: V.C. Sesacharri at the Press of Natesan [Vol. 1: Īśa, Kena, and Muṇḍaka: S.S. Sastri, 1898; second edition, 1905; Vol. 2: Kaṭha and Praśna: Sastri, 1898; Vol. 3-4: Chāndogya: Jha, 1899; Vol. 5: Aitareya and Taittirīya: Sastri, 1901].

Note: All volumes contain texts of the Upaniṣad and commentary and English translation.

8. Tattvabhusana, Sitanatha. The Upanisheds, edited with annotations and English translation. Two volumes. Calcutta: Som Brothers, 1900 and 1904.

9. Upaniṣadām Samuccayaḥ. Śrī-Nārāyaṇa-Śaṃkarānanda-viracita-dīpikā-sametānām Atharvaśikhādyānāṃ Haṃso-'paniṣad-antānāṃ dvātriṃśan-mitānām. Etat pustakam Ānandāśrama-stha-paṇḍitaiḥ sapāṭhāntara-nirdeśam saṃśodhitam. Puṇyākhya-pattane: Ānandāśrama-saṃskṛta-granthāvaliḥ. Granthāṅkaḥ 29 (second edition), 1925.

K. Translations: Collections

1. Lebail, P. Six Upanishads Majeures (Kena, Mundaka, Isha, Katha, Aitareya, Prashna). Paris, 1971.

2. Nikhilananda, Swami. Upaniṣads. London: Phoenix House and N.Y.: Harper Brothers [Selection 1: Kaṭha, Īśa, Kena, Muṇḍaka, 1951; Selection 2: Svetāśvatara, Praśna, Māṇḍukya, 1954; Selection 3: Aitareya and Bṛhadāraṇyaka, 1957; Selection 4: Taittirīya and Chāndogya, 1959].

3. Röer, E. The Twelve Principal Upaniṣads. Three volumes. Adyar, Madras: Theosophical Publishing House, 1931 [text in Devanāgarī, translation with notes in English from the Commentaries of Śaṅkarācārya and the Gloss of Ānandagiri. Vol. I: Īśa, Kena, Kaṭha, Praśna, Muṇḍaka, Māṇḍukya, Taittirīya, Aitareya, Śvetāśvatara; Vol. II: Bṛhadāraṇyaka Upaniṣad; Vol. III: Chāndogya and Kauṣītakī Upaniṣads].

4. Viraraghavachariar, Sri. Īśa, Kena, Kaṭha Upaniṣads. Ubhaya Vedānta Grantha Mālā 1-3.